RETIREMENT
SUCCESS

RETIREMENT SUCCESS

HIRING YOUR FUNCTIONAL RETIREMENT ADVISOR

JOSEPH F. FALBO, JR., CFP®

CONTENTS

INTRODUCTION

"An investment in knowledge pays the best interest."

- Benjamin Franklin

THE AVERAGE PERSON retiring in the 21st century has no idea of the challenges that await them in their "second life." They have worked hard and have diligently saved to accomplish their end goal—a comfortable, stress-free retirement. However, retirement isn't just about sipping piña coladas on the beach; in fact, the most crucial part of your fiscal responsibility starts now. But where to begin?

The first step—and the most important—is to find a Functional Retirement Advisor (FRA). This is a trustworthy, empathetic person who puts emphasis on plans not products. This advisor cares just as much about the QUALitative (knowing you as a person) aspects of your life as they do about the QUANTitative (the numbers). This is someone who, through years of experience and education, understands behavioral investing and applies these principles to their own financially secure life. It is my belief and my own experience that Functional Retirement Advisors need both QUANtitative and QUALitative data to create a precise and well-defined PLAN for you.

This book will help retirees recognize this advisor through an interview or two without relying solely on confusing, long-winded, burdensome rules. The reader can refer back to this book as well, and over time they will attune their "gut" and know the Functional Retirement Advisor intuitively.

You deserve to have a well-rounded, self-supporting and honorable retirement. With a dysfunctional advisor, you will have a dysfunctional retirement that leaves you dependent and undignified, relying on your children and the government to bail you out. With a Functional Retirement Advisor in place, you will have the greatest probability of achieving that comfortable, stress-free retirement you always dreamed of.

My aim was to make this book as short as possible. Why? Because I know that anything with brief instructions actually gets done and actually gets used. I believe that long-winded teachings just turn people off. I designed this book to be quick, easy and to the point.

Let me begin by explaining that a Functional Retirement Advisor is not a title or designation that can be attained or conferred upon a financial advisor. This is my own description of a skilled, long-term, industry-trained financial professional. A Functional Retirement Advisor makes sure they understand YOU. I am partial to the FRA because I've been a financial advisor since 1995 and have seen the good planning that the FRA can do for retirees.

I compare Functional Retirement Advisors to the physicians who practice functional medicine. Functional medicine treats the person who has the disease, not just the disease the person has. They go deeper and treat patients holistically, trying first to diagnose the "how" and the "why" of the illness, and then deciding "where do we go from here?" in treating their patients for the long term and getting them back on the right track, healthwise. The Functional Retirement Advisor advises the client (patient) and helps them get back on the right track, wealthwise.

Recognizing and then hiring your FRA is your BEST chance for overcoming the challenges of 21st-century retirement. Indeed, a quality relationship with an FRA may very well be the difference between a functional retirement and a dysfunctional retirement.

CHAPTER 1

WHY DO YOU REALLY NEED A FUNCTIONAL RETIREMENT ADVISOR?

"Our goals can only be reached through a vehicle of a plan in which we must fervently believe, and upon which we must vigorously act. There is no other route to success."

—*Pablo Picasso*

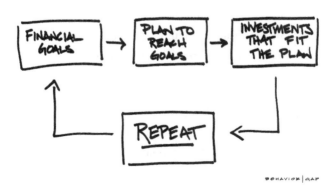

I believe you will want to be a good steward of your money and, therefore, you will want to hire a competent Functional Retirement Advisor. I recommend that people must find this type of advisor. This is a VERY important decision. They say marriage is one of the most important decisions you will make in your life, and they are right—it is. Maybe the number-one decision. But money decisions are very important too, and who you get your financial advice from is just as paramount. Here is the usual pecking order of things that are most meaningful to people: God (if you believe), health, then marriage/family and, money is right up there with them. Because of this scenario, I believe it is imperative for the vast majority of people to have a kind, empathetic, caring, competent, encouraging, preferably independent financial advocate. I mention preferably independent because I would like this financial advocate to be an independent advisor separate from the large broker dealers and banks. The reason I say this is, briefly speaking, all of the wirehouses (which are large, integrated brokerage firms with a national presence) are always looking to increase their profit margins. Sometimes these behemoths do things like pressure the advisor about meeting certain sales quotas. In that environment, it sometimes forces the advisor to take on more clients than they can handle or to look for products that increase revenue for the firm. This all makes it harder to establish a truly personal experience with their clients. However, I will say that it all depends on the individual advisor. Therefore, if it is an advisor employed by a wirehouse you are dealing with and they meet the five must-have criteria in this book (chapter 7), I would consider them a Functional Retirement Advisor as well.

I would like to put the power of being able to make

confident financial decisions into the clients' hands by helping them to become educated consumers. Yes, I believe in being educated about products and strategies, but this book is not about that. In addition to outlining how to recognize a Functional Retirement Advisor, I explain how to find a fiduciary (an advisor that puts your interests before their own interests) without having all the onerous fiduciary rules that make some advisors afraid to recommend investments to you for fear of being sued.

You won't need to have the burden of understanding the entire financial landscape of investments and strategies if you are in the capable hands of a Functional Retirement Advisor that you have complete confidence in. They already have this knowledge and expertise—that's what you are paying them for. The key is that they need to apply it correctly to your particular wants, needs, goals and intentions within your particular circumstances. You may even have dealings with an advisor who fits a lot of the criteria of a Functional Retirement Advisor; and you may feel you already have the most important piece—trust. Just as in any relationship, without trust there is no relationship. This is also true with an advisor–client relationship. I understand that it's hard to build this necessary ingredient of trust, but if you already have faith in an advisor you are comfortable with, then you're ahead of the game. I have some techniques to help you bring your priorities and needs to the forefront, which will also help your trusted advisor tie your money to your life. This is a piece that most advisors miss out on—perhaps they don't have an intentional way of going about gathering this information from you. Read the three questions by George Kinder later in this chapter and bring them to the advisor you already trust. Say to the advisor, "I want you to understand my situation, understand me as a person, my hopes, dreams and fears, so that you can set up my plan and investments toward the answers I have compiled to these three questions." Giving your answers to the advisor will strengthen their understanding of you as a person which should, in turn, help them to help you by having your plan geared to who YOU are.

Functional Advisor vs. Dysfunctional Advisor

"All financial success comes from acting on a plan. A lot of financial failure comes from reacting to the market."

—Nick Murray

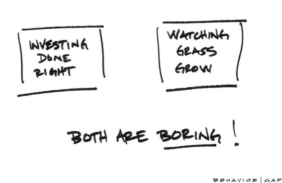

Neither you, your FRA nor anyone else on this planet can predict with accuracy and consistency short-term moves in economies or the timing of good and bad markets. (Any advisor saying they can—BIG RED FLAG.) Dysfunctional advisors as well as dysfunctional clients try to do this.

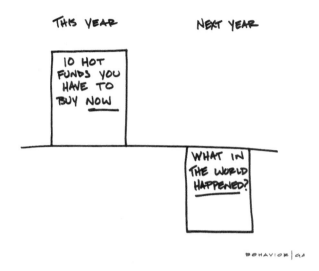

Successful investing is not about picking the best mutual fund or index, either. Just because some mutual fund or investment did very well the last year or three doesn't mean it's going to continue to do well. A Functional Retirement Advisor starts with a plan, has your investments well-diversified and is patient, and they have the discipline to act toward your plan based on your individual wants, needs, goals and intentions within your circumstances. If your long-term goals have not changed, the FRA will counsel you to not change your plan. A dysfunctional advisor or dysfunctional client, meanwhile, will push for these changes because they are so worried about what's going on in the markets and the economy. Therefore, they are obsessed about the performance of their funds.

Performance Verses Reaching Your Goals

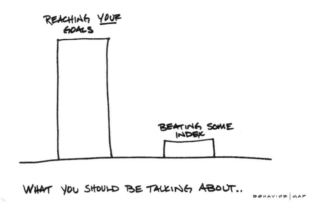

REACHING YOUR GOALS

BEATING SOME INDEX

WHAT YOU SHOULD BE TALKING ABOUT..

BEHAVIOR GAP

I am not talking about the advisor's "track record" or their performance. We live in the conventional wisdom of investing, which is all about market timing and is performance driven. That's what the TV and media teach us about investing and about financial advisors. That is the perception.

In reality, all successful investing is based on working toward your goals through a plan—patience and discipline are the reality. All unsuccessful investing is based on performance and market timing.

One of the difficult tasks for advisors is taking the time to get to know clients as people. This means asking questions that really don't focus on money as part of their data-gathering process. Many clients do not understand why it is so important and basically "mail it in" when it comes to answering advisors' questions about them as people, and often the client just winds up concentrating on the QUANtitative data—the money. This is what I and many other advisors experience when choosing the path of understanding clients as people.

The Functional Retirement Advisor who chooses to practice holistically in this way already understands it will lead to a win-win relationship. Because of this, the client will be open to trust the advisor's recommendations and to provide the much-needed QUALitative data (getting to know clients as people) in a trusted setting. Typically clients are apprehensive about sharing a more personal outlook with their advisors. However, once this QUALitative data is in a trusted Functional Retirement Advisor's able hands, we have what I call a natural-born financial fiduciary relationship.

Lowdown on QUANtitative and QUALitative Data

"Judge a man by his questions rather than by his answers."

— Voltaire

- *Why is money important to you?*

- *Why are you doing this planning?*

- *Why did you work so hard and sacrifice to save?*

- *What is your purpose, meaning and intention?*

QUANtitative data is the money. The numbers. Age is a number as well—think quantity, because you can measure how much. Obviously, dollar amounts, return percentages and cash flow needs are all QUANtitative. Most advisors do a good job getting QUANtitative. THINK QUANTITY—numbers. It is quantifiable.

Now, to get to the bottom of the why behind your planning we need QUALitative data. These are the more subjective questions your FRA will ask you. It is more values-based and depends on the person. What is the client's past investment experience? Did they have a bad experience with an investment advisor? It gives us a VISION: a reason for doing all the number stuff. Answering what's important about money to you is QUALitative. Think QUALITY—values. Goals that are relevant to you. Hopes, fears and values. Client's expectations. How is your health? Is it QUALitative? Health is qualitative and it is important. Tell me about your family. Tell me about the home you live in. Your work? All QUALitative.

BEHAVIOR | GAP

A Functional Retirement Advisor makes sure they under-stand YOU. Not only do they understand the figures but they also get to understand your individuality. Most advisors, especially Functional Retirement Advisors, are very good at handling money and advising on your current and future monetary situation. It is similar to going to a doctor: Most doctors are good at knowing symptoms and figuring out, with the use of technology, what the actual illness or injury is. However, they should know your QUALitative information too—for example, if you're an active runner, how often do you exercise, how much water do you drink a day, what kind of foods do you eat, what times of day do you eat, how much alcohol do you consume. (The doctor should actually have you make a food journal and go over with you what kinds of food you are eating daily). What kind of supplements do you take, if you take probiotics, Are you taking enough vitamin D, what do you want to be doing, what do you feel like, how tired are you, how do you sleep, what stresses you out, if you meditate, whether you walk, how long do you sit per day... etc., etc. Yes, they are already getting the other quantifiable information, such as medications you are on as well as your past medical records, if you are allergic to anything, your height, weight, blood pressure and pulse. This is a sound practice and what most doctors are doing. But are they going the extra mile in understanding you as a person with individual circumstances? This extra understanding would help you to get the most optimal health possible. (Note that it does not guarantee optimal health, but it gives you the best chance at achieving this).

What is 'Risk Tolerance'

Risk Tolerance

is the degree of *variability* in investment returns that an investor is willing to withstand.

Risk tolerance is an important component in *investing*. You should have a realistic understanding of your ability and willingness to stomach large *swings* in the value of your investments; if you take on too much risk, you might panic and sell at the wrong time

Risk tolerance could be either QUANtitative or QUALitative. You can use a numbered approach to it, by answering a questionnaire, but if your emotions get the best of you based on past experiences, it could be different. I would say that assessing risk tolerance is both. If risk tolerance is assessed just by talking to the client based on experience, it is QUALitative as long as the advisor discusses risk and the range of the risk. This way the client knows what to expect to a certain extent. Surprises can cause a dysfunctional retirement. An FRA helps you to prepare for both the expected and the unexpected.

Let's also buck the trend of seeing the QUANtitative (the numbers, the money) data as being more important than QUALitative data (knowing clients as people first). Most advisors and clients begin their conversations talking about the QUANtitative data. Yes, QUANtitative data is important data and needed data; however, we need to tie the money to the people and their lives. The three questions from George kinder of the kinder institute on page 15 are perfect examples of eliciting QUALitative data.

Life Planning: George Kinder— What You Can Learn From The Kinder Institute

"If you don't design your own life plan, chances are you'll fall into someone else's plan; and guess what they have planned for you? Not much."

—Jim Rohn (1930–2009), author and speaker.

BEHAVIOR|GAP

Internationally recognized as the father of the Life Planning movement, Harvard-educated George Kinder is the founder of the Kinder Institute of Life Planning. He has been a practicing financial planner and tax advisor for over 30 years. The Kinder Institute trainings are recognized worldwide as the standard for trainings in client-advisor relationship skills. You can find out more by visiting www.kinderinstitute.com.

In my career I have always instinctively known and practiced to learn about clients as people first before doing their financial planning. When I hired consultant Barry LaValley (discussed later in the book), he helped me understand the practice of formal financial life planning. But I was craving more education on the topic, so I searched for the top life planning expert and found George.

I signed up for George Kinder's *Seven Stages of Money Maturity* course held for financial advisors in Chicago where I learned how deeply rooted our emotions are tied to money. Then I did the week-long, intensive EVOKE course in Massachusetts. Here we went through all the steps, paired up with other advisors and conducted formal financial life plans on each other—a truly fantastic experience. The final piece of my journey in becoming a Registered Life Planner (RLP) with The Kinder Institute was a six-month internship which consisted of writing case studies and submitting them for the other apprentices to critique. This is similar to the way Harvard teaches students and is an amazing way to learn, as the feedback is invaluable.

According to Kinder, we need to attach meaning to our money—the unique purpose of our money. A mistaken perception is that money is just about numbers. Money is tied to our emotions, and the process of simply asking three questions, like Kinder's, along with other questions and discussing them with your Functional Retirement Advisor is mutually rewarding for both parties. I suggest you read Kinder's book, *Seven Stages Of Money Maturity*, and take a moment to think about the two experience questions that follow, because they are for you to think about internally.

Recall your first painful experience with money and your first joyful memory about money—how do they make you feel? Emotional? Do you happen to see any correlation in how you view money today? Most advisors and accountants do not help their clients with the emotional aspects concerning money. Your Functional Retirement Advisor, however, will be there for you.

The Three Questions

"But in the end, financial decisions aren't about getting rich. They're about getting what you want—getting happy."

— Carl Richards,
The Behavior Gap

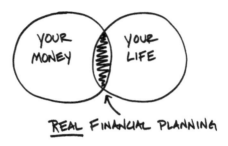

REAL FINANCIAL PLANNING

BEHAVIOR GAP

Kinder believes that life planning is essential to developing a sound financial plan. "Without life planning," he said during a talk at a recent conference, "Financial planning is like using a blunt instrument on the organism we call the human being."

I've argued before that the road to wealth is paved with goals. This is a similar sentiment—but it's not the same. Kinder isn't simply asking us to set goals; he's asking us to carefully examine our values, and thoughtfully decide what's important. To help clients discover the deeper values in their lives, Kinder poses three questions (These are the three questions we mentioned on page 3. Take some time to answer these questions and bring the results to discuss with your trusted advisor):

1. Imagine you are financially secure, that you have enough money to take care of your needs, now and in the future. How would you live your life? Would you change anything? Let yourself go. Don't hold back on your dreams. Describe a life that is complete and richly yours.

2. Now imagine that you visit your doctor, who tells you that you have only five to ten years to live. You won't ever feel sick, but you will have no notice of the moment of your death. What will you do in the time you have remaining? Will you change your life, and if so, how will you do it? (Note that this question does not assume unlimited funds.)

3. Finally, imagine that your doctor shocks you with the news that you only have 24 hours to live. Notice what feelings arise as you confront your very real mortality. Ask yourself: What did you miss? Who did you not get to be? What did you not get to do?[1]

This material was developed by George Kinder and the Kinder Institute of Life Planning. It is part of a program of trainings that lead to the Registered Life Planner® designation. Used by permission of George Kinder © 1999

Kinder says that answering the first question is easy. There are lots of things we would do if money were no

---

1 *https://www.kinderinstitute.com*

object. But as the questions progress, there's a sort of funnel. They become more difficult to answer, and there are fewer possible responses. Life planning is all about answering the third question.

Who are you? How do you find out who you are? And how can you let your advisor know who you are? The answers help them to tie your money to your life and to bring meaning and purpose to this money that you are both cognizant of.

Product Dump

I had an experience recently with a prospective client—I was explaining how we get to know our clients as people first and then talk about the money. I said to him, "We need to start with a financial plan based on your individual wants, needs, goals and circumstances. I cannot put a good plan together without knowing you as a person. Once we have this, I can then use all my knowledge and experience to put you in the right strategies and opportunities to get you to where you want to go." The very next words out of the client's mouth were, "What products do you offer?" and "What is your track record?" He then proceeded to show me his statements and said, "Here is what I am invested in, do you have better products for me?" Me: "I don't know. Did you even tell me what you are trying to accomplish yet?"

I blame the financial industry for financial advisors and clients who start and end financial-planning conversations only by discussing the numbers. Through no fault of their own, clients are actually expecting a product dump as a result of generations of abusive sales practices. This is what gives the Fiduciary Rule some steam and legitimacy. The Fiduciary Rule is the "best-interest" rule, which we get into more in the next chapter. It is a giant cesspool of a rule that is proposed, which, if implemented, would bring so much more red tape to the financial industry.

I see newspaper articles by some financial news columnists (who, by the way, hate financial advisors to begin with) that talk about asking your advisor to sign a best-interest contract that says the advisor is a fiduciary. This means the advisor is legally bound to put your best interest first. You can't make this up! You mean to tell me that if the advisor does not want to put your best interest first, signing this paper will break him down and force him to? I am still waiting to hear exactly how they are going to enforce this! ::*CRICKETS*::

Also, I must emphasize: There is nothing wrong with selling and buying products—it just depends on whether you need them or not. And this is what your Functional Retirement Advisor can help you with. That's why you start with a plan so your advisor gets to know you as a person first.

Dysfunctional Fee-based Advisors and Dysfunctional Commission-based Advisors

One such financial asset that has strong opinions for and against it is an annuity.

Annuity

An annuity, in its simplest terms, is a financial contract written by an insurance company that provides for a series of guaranteed payments, either for a specified period of time or the lifetime of one or more individuals.

However, they are much more complex than this and come in all types. That definition basically defines an immediate annuity. But there are also deferred, fixed, fixed-indexed and variable annuities that have all sorts of different nuances. Because of the variety and complexity of each type of annuity, it is a discussion you would need to have with your FRA to determine if you or they believe it would be in your best interest to own one. Now, there are some people out there (including dysfunctional, fee-based advisors) that bash annuities, and then there are others (including dysfunctional, commission-only advisors) that only sell annuities. Whether to own these or not is all based on your financial condition, but just make sure your advisor is taking your best interests to heart.

Some thoughts to consider: What are these annuities going to do for you? Why are you doing this? What is the strategy? How does this benefit you? What does this investment do for you emotionally speaking? How does it tie to your life?

This does not mean the advisors using annuities are bad at what they do, or that annuities are to be avoided like the plague. Sometimes they make sense for people. They can be a great tool when used in the right context for the right type of client who is looking for what an annuity provides.

Annuities are way beyond the scope of this book, but I will say some have high costs but give benefits for that cost; some are lower-cost. It could be okay if they are higher-cost as long as you, as a client, see the value in it. Know why you are doing it and what they are doing for you and what you are paying for. During the 2009 market downturn, some of my clients held different types of annuities (where it made sense for them), and they were able to deal with the downturn much better than most of their friends. It drives me nuts when fee-only advisors bash them. Some people really need them. Of course, some people do not need them, and yes there are advisors that are only doing annuities for the commissions. Again, it's a smaller percentage of advisors doing this—but that ain't right, either. So that's why you need to be working with the Functional Retirement Advisor.

CHAPTER 2

WHAT IS THE FIDUCIARY RULE? WHY DO YOU NEED TO KNOW ABOUT IT?

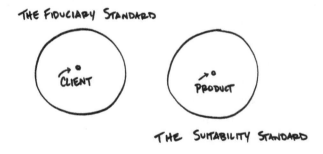

THE FIDUCIARY STANDARD

CLIENT

PRODUCT

THE SUITABILITY STANDARD

BEHAVIOR | GAP

I've been talking about it—The Fiduciary Rule. Before we get into it, I would like to point out that I am obviously a big proponent of advisors putting clients' interests before their own. This is what advisors are supposed to be doing automatically; that's what this book is all about. I honestly cannot believe that it has gotten to this, where the government has to step in to regulate it.

But I digress. Let's define what a fiduciary is.

Fiduciary relationship

one person, in a position of vulnerability, justifiably vests confidence, good faith, reliance and trust in another whose aid, advice or protections is sought in some matter. In such a relationship, good conscience requires the fiduciary to act at all times for the sole benefit and interest of the one who trusts.

The Department of Labor (DOL) fiduciary rule forces all financial advisors to be required to recommend what is in the best interest of clients when they offer guidance on 401(k) plans, individual retirement accounts or other qualified monies saved for retirement. Many broker-dealers who currently operate under a less stringent suitability standard that only requires investment advice to be appropriate (and doesn't necessarily have to be in your best interest) have already been crafting new administrative steps and investing millions in technology and training to meet the rule's requirements. The DOL rule requires advisors who accept commissions or revenue sharing to have their clients sign a best interest contract exemption, or BICE. This is a pledge that the adviser will act in their client's best interest and only earn "reasonable" compensation. It discloses information to clients about fees and conflicts of interest. Under the DOL fiduciary rule, investors with BICE contracts in place are able to sue their advisors in court if they believe their interests have not come first.[2]

Using all of the reasons above, proponents of the rule say this is good for the industry and for the clients. Opponents to the rule say that there are many unintended consequences. They argue that it will bring down the quality of investment advice because it encourages litigation over financial recommendations, which is a very subjective matter. For example, even defining what a "best interest" standard means in concrete terms is not easy. The courts will wind up deciding this definition on an ongoing, case-by-case basis, which can throw the financial industry into (even more) chaotic confusion.

Case in point, look at the NFL "Catch Rule." You don't have to be a sports fan to appreciate this analogy. Because the NFL has been unable to define what a "fair catch" is in concrete terms, teams have lost games and even championships because individual referees have differing opinions on what influences their "fair catch" rulings. One referee in a given game may call a catch made in the corner of the end zone a touchdown, but in the next game, the same player could make the same exact catch only to be ruled out of bounds by a different referee. In other words, the NFL's uncertainty on this subjective matter has become highly controversial. They also keep releasing different rules over the years on what a catch is to simplify it, yet it continues to create complications.

As a result, advisors may be afraid to offer certain financial strategies for fear of winding up in a court room. What

2 http://www.investmentnews.com/article/20160509/FEA-TURE/160509939/the-dol-fiduciary-rule-will-forever-change-financial-advice-and-the

this may mean for you is, because the advisor is walking on egg shells, you may not be getting the best of their knowledge, experience and "gut instincts" in dealing with your overall financial plan. Opponents also say it unnecessarily drives up the cost and time to the point that advisers are less likely to take on clients with smaller accounts.

The good news is that the threat of the DOL rule has already influenced the current watchdogs of the financial industry with heightened fiduciary awareness. For instance, the Securities and Exchange Commission (SEC), which is the primary federal regulatory agency for the securities industry, and the Financial Industry Regulatory Authority, Inc. (FINRA), a private corporation that acts as a self-regulatory organization, have swayed broker-dealers to lower commissions to DOL-level approved rates. Further, the SEC and FINRA have been evolving their regulatory practices over the past decade with advanced technology, such as data analytics, aimed to rule out fraud.

No one knows if the DOL ruling will be implemented since during the time of this writing the Fifth Circuit Court of Appeals has vacated the whole rule. The Department of Labor has some time to either ask the court to look at the case again or it can appeal to the Supreme Court—or they will just let it fizzle out. Not a soul knows if the DOL ruling will move forward, or, if it were to be enforced, would anyone know if the long term consequences would be positive or negative. Beyond the DOL rule, there are also talks of the SEC coming out with its own version of the fiduciary rule. And around and around we go…

My point is, whether this goes through or not, using the

methods in this book will surpass any ruling. The reason I say this is because the advisors with bad intent (the ones who can't even spell the word "fiduciary" never mind abide by its terms—remember Bernie Madoff was a fiduciary) won't respect any kind of "rule" and will do what they want anyway. Or, the other type of dysfunctional advisor—a person whose heart may be in the right place, but offers subpar financial planning solutions due to their lack of Functional Retirement Advisor (FRA) criteria—won't suddenly start dishing out competent advice because their signature appears on a piece of paper saying they promise to put your best interests first. By doing your own homework, you can do a far better job at sniffing out a true fiduciary much more proficiently than any government or agency pencil pusher.

The DOL Rule has also brought fees to the forefront, and this chatter has already lowered many unnecessary fees in the industry. But any kind of ruling shouldn't be laser focused on cheapening financial advice; it should be about getting better quality services for clients. A Functional Retirement Advisor wants to be paid fairly for his or her money management skills. They deserve it, and you want this, because when an FRA is paid fairly, they are imbedded in your success and your success is their success. It's a win-win. Unfortunately, many people can be penny wise and dollar foolish.

I see financial advisors who market themselves as fiduciaries that are willing to sign a piece of paper that attests that they will put your best interest first. *Thanks, guys: You are amazing! The clients should really be jumping in there now that you will sign for that!* Or I see advertisements for some advisors explaining that they are "fee only"—as if being paid by fees is going to make them guarantee they will work with your best interest in mind or even be competent for that matter.

Remember, It Is About PREVENTION

"Prevention is better than cure."

— *Desiderius Erasmus*

Working with an advisor who meets my criteria (FRA) is a preventative measure. This gives you a much greater chance, in my experience, of having a true fiduciary. The fiduciary rules that are outlined by the SEC, FINRA and even the DOL is about after the fact. The financial advisor signs a form saying that he is a fiduciary. Later on, for whatever reason, you feel that he is not a fiduciary .... Now what? Who wants all the ugliness of suing them? If it's going to end that way, let's not start that way. This book is about *prevention*.

Stack the Deck in Your Favor

"Live life as if everything is stacked in your favor"

— Rumi

There is always a need for reasonable rules and regulations, but at reasonable levels. The more important take away for you is that the best and most rational way of going about making sure you have an advisor with your best interests in mind is to make sure you *have a good* financial advisor. Of course, nothing is perfect: Just because they hit all the characteristics in this book does not guarantee you a 100%

success rate of having an advisor who is proficient and has your best interests before their own. Then again, what is guaranteed 100% in this life? I can actually hear you saying it—*yup*—death and taxes. *However*, hitting all the characteristics in this book—the criteria—*will heavily* stack the deck in your favor that you indeed will have a natural-born fiduciary guiding you through the 21st-century retirement.

Conclusion: Please don't let this rule lull you into a false sense of security if it goes through or have fear if it does not go through. You still need to be an active participant in your money management, and that means first and foremost finding an FRA.

Remember, an FRA is *always* a fiduciary, a fiduciary is *not always* an FRA.

Fee Justification? $100 on Coffee?

"Price is what you pay. Value is what you get."

— *Warren Buffett*

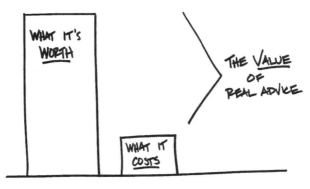

According to a recent article in *Business Insider* about fee justification,[3] "If you pay $100 for anything—investment advice, coffee, or child care—that's $100 you will no longer have to invest for retirement. In other words, buy any item and that amount of money, plus years of compounding, will be removed from your potential retirement assets and future income. Choosing not to pay $100 a month for coffee, or $155 for a cell plan with unlimited texting, or $189 for cable, or $750 for a monthly BMW lease would free up a pile of money that could go into your portfolio and improve your current retirement savings and ultimate income in retirement. And none of those things will help you manage your financial affairs any better. By focusing solely on how expenses and fees can impact a portfolio, you are ignoring whether you are receiving any value for the dollars you spend on financial advice."A recently updated Vanguard study attributed very little investment performance benefit to working with an advisor. But what it did find was that investors did obtain broad benefits from the planning, portfolio construction and wealth-management process, and especially from behavioral coaching offered by a skillful advisor.[4]

Vanguard's study indicated that an advisor who is helping a client find and use lower-cost investment tools can add nearly 0.5% to long-term performance, managing asset allocations between taxable and nontaxable accounts can add up to 0.75%, intelligent rebalancing can add 0.35%

---

3 http://www.businessinsider.com/paying-for-a-financial-adviser-worth-it-2016-10

4 http://www.businessinsider.com/vanguard-personal-advisor-services-review

and thoughtful withdrawal strategies can add another 0.7%. Some people pay a small fortune nursing their coffee habit but scoff at the notion of paying a fee for financial advice.[5]

By far the biggest value was realized from an advisor helping clients write, understand and stick to their financial plan. Behavioral advice alone can add 1.5% to a client's long-term performance, according to Vanguard's study. Are you really a sitting target, as the financial journalists, media and advertisements say, by paying 1% per year for advice that may improve your long-term outcome by as much as 3% per year?

Your FRA is able to help you with questions such as: Which account should you draw on first in retirement? When should you take Social Security? Should you take your lump sum payment or take the pension (stream of payments for life) option?

How will you factor in all the different variables? When you have a question—any question—who will you trust? And who will ask you the hard questions when your investment behavior threatens to derail your long-term financial plans? You trust your Functional Retirement Advisor!

Anecdotally, think about this health analogy: It shouldn't be about getting "cheap" medical care, it should be about getting *good* medical care at good prices. This book puts the power in the client's hands. Yes, you should understand the fees, and yes, you should understand your investments, but after all—the reason you are hiring an investment advisor is because they did the schooling, they

---

5 www.ThomsonReuters.com

have the experience of dealing with all different types of situations, economies and the client's life transitions. They went to school for this, attended numerous workshops, and completed hours upon hours of continuing education, coaching, private training and accreditations to stay on top of their field (and I am speaking from experience here).

CHAPTER 3

THE LANDSCAPE OF THE 21ST-CENTURY RETIREMENT

"People know what they are retiring from, but they don't know what they are retiring to."

— Barry LaValley, Founder of
The Retirement Lifestyle Center

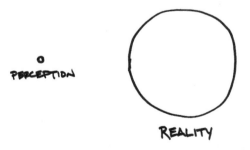

FUTURE FINANCIAL NEEDS

o
PERCEPTION

REALITY

BEHAVIOR|GAP

The 21st-century retirement is not our parent's or grand-parent's "The Greatest Generation" retirement. I am going to keep this part short because you might have heard this in some variation; if not, you know this instinctively.

People are living longer—and, in fact, much longer. The average retiree is going to live 20 to 30 years in retirement, and medical science is getting smarter and helping to extend life. Also, people don't realize that in the next 20 to 25 years, they may expand life-span exponentially from what we know today. This is wonderful news, especially if they can help with the quality of life as well. However, for a newly-minted retiree at 65 years old there is a major challenge—inflation. I won't even go in to all the numbers on inflation (the raising of prices of the things we buy) over a 20-25 to, who knows? possibly 40 years or more retirement period; I will leave that to your Functional Retirement Advisor. If you want to quickly see how much things cost and how inflation affects us, look up the price of houses in your area 30 years ago, then check today's price of the houses in your area. Or, check out an average car 30 years ago. At the time of this writing, an average car (I'm not talking luxury) in 2017 was $26,000 to $30,000. Back in 1987, an average car—for example, a Chevrolet Camaro—was approximately $10,409 for the basic sport coupe model.

Are you understanding this challenge? Which way do you think prices of the goods you buy will go over your 20-, 30- or possibly 40-year and beyond retirement life? Up or down? Up…you know this already. I am just merely pointing it out. Not to pile on, but how about medical costs? Just because you are on Medicare doesn't mean you aren't shelling out a lot of money. If you are over 65 years old, you know what I am talking about; if you are not...WAIT and see. If health care costs plus catastrophic illness are not in your retirement plan, you have a HUGE hole in your bucket. And by the way, medical costs are not going down—as a matter of fact, they are going up at a rate that's more than the average cost of living. The average cost of living went up approximately 2-3% a year on average over the last 80 years or so. You can see how much health care inflation is outpacing the Consumer Price Index (regular inflation) on the chart on page 34.

Rising health care costs are attributable to an overreliance on hospital care. Add all of Medicare's hospital costs to that, and further add emergency room treatment, which is very expensive, and you have one-third of all health care costs in America. By 2011, there were 136 million emergency room visits. An astonishing one out of five adults uses the emergency room each year. A second cause of rising health care costs is an epidemic of preventable health crises. The four leading causes of this crisis are heart disease, cancer, chronic obstructive pulmonary disorder and stroke. Chronic conditions cause all of them. That means they can either be prevented or would cost less to treat if caught in time. Risk factors for heart disease and strokes are poor nutrition and obesity. Smoking is a risk factor for lung cancer (the most common type) and COPD. Obesity is also a risk factor for the other common forms of cancer.

These diseases cost an extra $7,900 each; that's five times more than the costs for a healthy person! The average cost of treating diabetes, for example, is $26,971 per family. These diseases are difficult to manage because patients get tired of taking the various medications. Those who cut back often find themselves in the emergency room with heart attacks, strokes and other complications.[6]

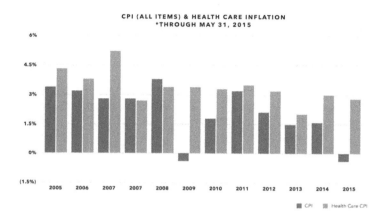

Source: Forbes, June 29, 2015 US Healthcare
Costs Rise Faster Than Inflation
(left side bars represent CPI and right side
bars represent Health Care CPI)

What's even worse, retiring baby boomers will more than double Medicare and Medicaid costs by 2020. As health care costs increase faster than economic growth, Medicare taxes and the Medicare Trust Fund will cover less and less. By 2030, the Trust Fund will be bankrupt, and taxes will only pay for 48% of the costs.

Listen, if you just do something stupid and die 10 minutes into retirement—*congratulations, you made it!*—financially

---

6 "The Impact of Chronic Diseases on Health Care," For a Healthier America, 2014.

speaking, that is. BUT, what if you live longer than people are expecting to live, with all the medical miracles and advances we will see over the next two or three decades?

Flash back to the Greatest Generation. Generally speaking, our parents and grandparents lived, on average, 10 to 15 years in retirement. They had pensions, which is basically a salary from the government or from the company where you used to work that you receive from the day you retire until the day you die. They also had Social Security benefits. Not that I think Social Security is going anywhere, but don't you think these benefits may be negatively impacted for people who have saved money for retirement? I do! They call this possible negative impact to people's Social Security "means tested." Basically, that means at some point the government may say that if you have a certain amount of money, in earnings or savings, you will get a smaller Social Security check than was originally planned. In my opinion, if you are 60 years old or over, this should not affect you. Below 60 years old…prepare. You are forewarned, and it should be in your plan that you might not get full Social Security benefits. (Don't get mad at me, I didn't make this up—I am just the messenger, and this is a real possibility.) Most of our parents and grandparents, on average, did not need to hire an advisor because of the retirement landscape at the time during which they retired. Circumstances were different, and they did not need an inordinate amount of retirement financial planning to accomplish a sound retirement.

Fast-forward to today. Most of us have no pensions; and if you do have one, you are blessed—pray they last. There could be an avalanche with all the pension debt in this country that could cut pension benefits.

Let's talk about the vast majority of people these days who do not have pensions. In 1974, ERISA, the Employee Retirement Income Security Act, changed the rules on us. In 1978, the first cash deferral arrangement was added to pensions—the 401(k). A 401(k) is a retirement savings plan sponsored by an employer. It lets workers save and invest a piece of their paycheck before taxes are taken out. Taxes aren't paid until the money is withdrawn from the account. They were supplemental plans; but in the '90s pensions were frozen (an unintended consequence) and then eventually eliminated. Long story short, when the government changed the rules, private companies viewed pensions differently, and because of this replaced them with 401(k)s, 403(b)s etc. A 403(b) plan, also known as a tax-sheltered annuity plan, is a retirement plan for employees of specific tax-exempt organizations such as health care organizations and colleges and universities. Where is all the uncertainty when you have a pension? It's with the company. They are liable. They are on the hook to make sure that the money does not run out from the day you retire to the day you die. Where is all the uncertainty when you have a 401(k) or 403(b)? You got that right! On YOU!

So let me get this straight—baby boomers are living for twice the amount of time their parents lived in retirement, and it's going to get even longer. Every year in this long retirement the prices of goods and services we consume is going to go UP (if history is any guide). Social Security could get means-tested, and we have these 401(k)s or 403(b)s where all the danger is on – US? Yep. That's the breakdown, and very real reasons why even most people who live and breathe financial matters will NOT want to do it all on their

How to write a review on Amazon:

To submit a review:
1. Go to the www.Amazon.com
2. Sign in to Amazon using your id and password
3. Type in Retirement Success in the search field.
4. Click on customer review or scroll down to the reviews
5. Click **Write a customer review** in the Customer Reviews section.
6. Click **Submit**

own. Interesting points from the Centers for Disease Control (CDC) show that this information illustrates how longevity is a factor already today. According to its studies and data from the U.S. Census Bureau filed in the U.S., it was determined that death rates have been dropping for Americans of almost every age for decades now. Indeed, a study of Americans ages 100 years and older shows that although Americans in their very golden years are still rare, the population has grown by 44% in recent years, from 50,281 in 2000 to 72,197 in 2014.[7]

As we watch the time quickly pass us by over the next few decades, so will we see longevity increasing exponentially. This, of course, means we can expect to be retired longer. Consequently, we will need a good Functional Retirement Advisor to help us plan for rising capital needs during our functional retirement.

---

7 http://www.cnn.com/2016/01/25/health/centenarians-increase/index.html

CHAPTER 4

PROCRASTINATION

"One of these days I'm going to get help for my procrastination problem."

— Unknown

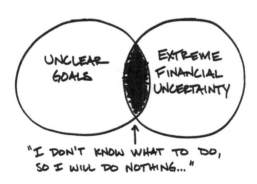

"I DON'T KNOW WHAT TO DO, SO I WILL DO NOTHING..."

BEHAVIOR | GAP

Just because you find a Functional Retirement Advisor, that doesn't mean you are guaranteed success. They cannot perform miracles. I am just saying this is your best chance to come out on top of the 21st-century retirement.

But first, let's talk about procrastination: why you procrastinate, and the negative impact it has.

According to *Psychological Science,* it is estimated that one-fifth of adults and half of all students procrastinate. Negative impacts of procrastination include diminished performance, poorer mental and physical health, and increased stress, worry and guilt. Longitudinal studies of procrastination have indicated that it "appears to be a self-defeating behavior pattern marked by short-term benefits and long-term costs."[8]

Psychology Today magazine explains that while more research remains to be done, researchers tend to agree that the reason why an individual procrastinates can vary idiosyncratically, and that the "cure" is to respond to whatever reasons might be specific for the individual.[9]

Here are a few reasons why you procrastinate on your retirement planning:

Reason: You've learned to procrastinate from role models. For example, your parents and/or grandparents have not done any retirement planning with an advisor. They possibly have not invested at all.

Suggestion: *Just by learning from this book about the issues and challenges we face in 21st century retirement should help to spur you toward your goals. Start by just writing down a*

---

8 Tice, Dianne M.; Baumeister, Roy F. (1997). Longitudinal study of procrastination, performance, stress and health: The costs and benefits of dawdling. Psychological Science 8.6, 454–458.

9 www.psychologytoday.com/blog/fearless-you/201506/9-reasons-you-procrastinate-and-9-ways-stop

goal or two that you would like to accomplish. If you really want to take charge, define what retirement success is to you. Write it out. Defining what a successful retirement looks like to you is the beginning of attaining that success. A great tool you can use to do this is in Chapter 1, where you can go ahead and answer George Kinder's three questions to help bring clarity and determine your vision of retirement.

Reason: You don't think you'll be effective at the task or don't even know how to do it. Retirement planning is overwhelming at first, especially since most people are not familiar with finance as it is.

Suggestion: *Try taking a few small steps at a time. It makes you feel good when you accomplish small tasks. For example, figure out your expenses first. Get your last six months of credit card statements, bank statements and checks written, and tally up what you have spent over the past six months. Then figure it into an annual and monthly number. Once you have expenses, another fantastic step is you can go to Chapter 13 where you* can learn how to go ahead and calculate your number. This would give you the actual lump sum dollar amount you will need in savings for retirement.

Reason: You don't want to spend the time doing it. Most of the investment and financial world is unknown to the rest of the world, so anxiety and discomfort is very normal. The fear of being judged on either your spending or your asset amount could be scary. It's like being "financially" naked in front of someone. Naturally, there is anxiety and discomfort.

Suggestion: *Taking small steps works here, too. Remember, you may think you are the only one with a certain issue that embarrasses you; however, the FRA has most likely seen your situation before. They are not there to judge you, they are paid to help you—to jump into your shoes, understand where you are now and where you want to be, and then help get you there.*

Reason: Your perfectionism gets in the way of moving ahead. You may be looking for the perfect investment or the perfect time to invest or how to complete the whole process perfectly.

Suggestion: *Remember, unfortunately nothing in this world is perfect. Even when you have a solid relationship with an FRA there will be some bumps in the road. Waiting for perfection is a recipe for disaster. Exactness goes out the window in the financial planning realm. A liberating way to take charge is figuring out your budget and making sure your spending habits are in line with your answers to George Kinder's three questions. (Your answers should help you set goals that motivate and intrigue you). As you go through your expenses, you can ask yourself the following questions: Is this expense in line* *with my lifetime goals and intentions? If not, is this expense necessary? Can it be swapped out for something else, reduced, or is it something you can completely do away with?*

Check out this website called You Need A Budget[10] at *www.ynab.com.* They have all sorts of information and webinars on how to master the art of budgeting which will help you take control of your money. Budgeting = Awareness!

Awareness

is the ability to directly know and perceive, to feel, or to be cognizant of events. More broadly, it is the state of being conscious of something.

Your Functional Retirement Advisor can gently nudge you in the right direction, but, ultimately, you must want to do the task yourself. There is an old adage: *Failing to Plan is Planning to Fail.*

---

10 www.ynab.com

CHAPTER 5

HYPERBOLIC FINANCIAL NEWS

"Conventional wisdom in Galbraith's view must be simple, convenient, comfortable and comforting - though not necessarily true."

— Steven D. Levitt, Freakonomics: A Rogue Economist Explores the Hidden Side of Everything

I hope you're not doing your own planning based on what is reported in the newspapers and all of the other 24-7 shameless financial news that is going on. News sells on fear. The number of people reading an article is what drives the news, and scary headlines are *always* what sells the most. Exaggerated news will always be 24-7, and they have to produce "news" so that people will watch every minute of the day.

News directors bring on "experts" who can give convincing reasons why the markets are going down and then others with convincing reasons why they are going up, all within the primary goal of putting on a good show—because, after all, it is television and there must be ratings. These "phony experts" are saying the end of the world is coming…especially in bad markets. The TV news is like The Weather Channel—showing you the storms, hurricanes and possibly asteroids speeding past our planet. These types of headlines and topics sell papers and programs, and they keep people glued to the TV, which helps them rake in advertising dollars. Do you think this is a formula that puts your best interests first?

Let me emphasize: You need a *plan,* but you can't make a plan out of what is being said on TV, because they have their own agenda and the message will change with the next commercial break. One reason this works in the media's favor is because most people expect investing to be exciting. It is not—the important solid principals of investing and retirement aren't exactly riveting.

The information you receive from the media may not necessarily be totally "false" news, but you don't necessarily want to base your retirement plan on it. It's their opinion, and they can't give good, clean advice for everybody— everybody's situation is unique.

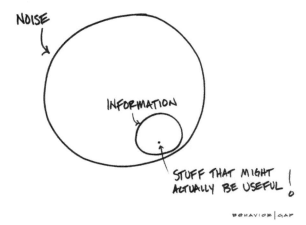

Don't Get Your Financial Advice from the Boob Tube

We all have retirement risk, but I see many examples of average, hardworking Americans who are getting their financial education from television show hosts. So let me get this straight—you are entertaining acting on advice regarding your retirement nest egg from a media personality who doesn't know you from a hole in the wall? I have often noticed that these shows are for people who haven't saved for retirement.

You will see questions on these shows like, "I have $30,000 in credit card debt. What should I do to get the interest rate down?" Or, "Should I roll my $2,000 Roth

IRA or not?" Or, "I have $100,000 in student loan debt and I'm not sure how to pay it off." The key point is: You cannot make a financial plan out of current happenings in the media. If you do, you will be stressed out and sorry in the long term. And for 21st-century retirement issues, you need solid, clean, *custom* advice from a Functional Retirement Advisor. Otherwise it is like putting a BANDAID® on a bullet wound. If you want to do it on your own for "cheap" I get it, and I say good luck to you. I just truly believe in my heart of hearts that you are up against great odds.

Be Aware of Spending Messages

Mixed messages are not only coming from financial pundits; they are coming from sources of entertainment. For example, look at the plight of *Real Housewives of New Jersey* stars Teresa and Joe Giudice. On the hit Bravo show, the couple was the epitome of the American Dream—beautiful homes, lavish getaways, fancy cars…all achieved on the shoulders of Joe, a hard-working Italian immigrant. Their life of glitz and glam was consumed by millions of fans who were transfixed by their cash-fueled exploits.

However, what you see on "reality" television does not always translate to real life. In 2014, Teresa and Joe were sentenced to 15 months and 41 months in prison, respectively, for *bank and bankruptcy fraud.* Joe was also accused of failing to file tax returns between 2004 and 2008, and faces deportation after his release (he is still serving out his sentence at the time of this book). It turned out their *Life of Riley* act was all smoke and mirrors.

Consumers are bombarded daily with examples of how "cool" it is to live beyond your means. These messages live in commercials, print advertisements, songs on the radio, social media "influencers" and more. These kinds of forces are keeping most of our countrymen from being prosperous; they prey on our inclination to "have fun" and spend impulsively. Most of the time, unconscious spending makes ourselves feel better or gives us a false sense of fitting in with our peers. Money is more psychological than it is about logic and numbers, and we must resist buying into the temptation of the Kardashian lifestyle in order to build and keep wealth.

CHAPTER 6

FINANCIAL EDUCATION IN OUR COUNTRY

FOREST

NO TREES

Americans are great at graduating from college, getting advanced degrees, becoming doctors, lawyers, engineers and teachers. However, there is poor financial education in this country. In high school and college, you are lucky if you so much learn how to balance a checkbook or prepare a budget. As we get older and the stakes get higher, not having true financial literacy (outside of learning from the example our parents have set) puts many in dire straits. That is why so many Americans turn to media outlets for their financial information which, as we learned in the last chapter, can give consumers false impressions. Sometimes—even worse—from friends or family....such as, the people that do it as a hobby, giving out part-time advice, most of the time not knowing the full situation of the person that they are giving advice to. In my experience, these "part-time advice givers"—you know, the brother-in-law who thinks he knows it all thanks to his subscription to *Money Magazine*—...yeah, that guy...these people know just about enough to be extremely dangerous. Do you get your medical recommendations from your friend the plumber, just because he's healthy? No, of course not. You would go to someone trained as a doctor, or if you believe in holistic medicine, a holistic doctor. If they are a functional medicine doctor, they would get to know you and your situation first before they would recommend what to do.

So we have lousy financial education coupled with all the challenges of the 21st-century retirement [living much longer, inflation, most of us have no pensions, we have 401(k)s], and who knows what's going on with Social Security and Medicare? Add to the equation investor behavioral issues (discussed in Chapter 13), and I just don't see how to do it without a Functional Retirement Advisor who puts your best interests first automatically.

Would you operate on your own heart? Would you change a transmission if you aren't a mechanic? Would you open your mouth wide and perform your own root canal? Better yet, would you ask your brother-in-law his advice on any of these three? Or would you look on YouTube on how to do it first? I believe your retirement planning should be held to the same high standards.

You don't go into 21st-century retirement on your own. Like I said, if you are going to do it yourself I wish you the best. It is simply too emotional to do it on your own. And why? Because your money is tied to your emotions—just don't forget that. I strongly recommend having a great relationship with a Functional Retirement Advisor.

CHAPTER 7

CRITERIA FOR
A FUNCTIONAL
RETIREMENT ADVISOR

"What you want in a mentor is someone who truly cares for you and who will look after your interests and not just their own. When you do come across the right person to mentor you, start by showing them that the time they spend with you is worthwhile."

—Vivek Wadhwa

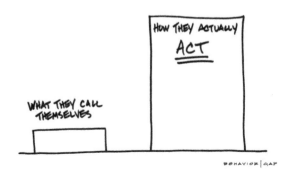

I am convinced these are the five areas of "must-have" characteristics to look for in a Functional Retirement Advisor:

1. Trust and empathy. The advisor gets to know the client as a person by gathering Quantitative *and* Qualitative data.

2. They must have at least 15 years of experience in financial planning for individuals.

3. The financial advisor has a financial plan for THEM-SELVES and are financially secure THEMSELVES.

4. They have a designation like a CFP, ChFC, etc.

5. They practice behavior management and behavior investing for at least part of the portfolio.

Your Functional Retirement Advisor naturally complements you and your family. A true, cohesive team that gels, they make 1 plus 1 equal 3. The late, great author Steven Covey (*7 Habits of Highly Effective People*) called it "synergy." Meaning, when solving issues, your group is often smarter than the smartest person within it and the result is exponentially superior. They make the family's situation better for having dealt with them. The above rules increase your chances of getting such an advisor. In addition, to the traits outlined above do not forget to look for an FRA that wants to start with a plan.

First impressions mean everything. When first hiring an advisor, I strongly advise meeting them in person or, at the very least, conducting a video conference call. I am ok with a long-distance relationship; I have many, and they work fine. I just want you to get a good feel for the advisor, especially when you are first hiring them. It is important to be able to look them in the eye and see their body language. This helps with getting a quality read on them, and it is the best way to determine whether you can truly trust this person. Incidentally, many low-cost/low-service providers will only communicate by telephone and e-mail.

One other thing to note is, typically, one advisor can only realistically work with about 200 relationships maximum by themselves. To service more than this number satisfactorily, they will need another full-time advisor on staff. Generally speaking, one advisor equates to being able to handle 200 relationships. Therefore, if you are dealing with an advisor that is servicing 500-1,000 relationships (this is the amount of clients many advisors working at large broker dealers, banks and low-cost service providers are engaging) it is virtually impossible for this advisor to know each individual on a personal level. You want to be sure you are working with them directly on major planning topics, and not an assistant.

You should be able to discover most of the five characteristics in the initial consultation or at least before signing up with them. Each of the five characteristics, are described in greater detail in the following chapters. They are the rules of thumb to know if you are dealing with the right person to help with your retirement nest egg, according to my experience of living and breathing this business for over two decades.

CHAPTER 8

TRUST & CONFIDENCE

"There is a voice that doesn't use words. Listen."

— Rumi

WHEN LOOKING FOR A
REAL ADVISOR

EMOTIONAL $>$ SALES
STABILITY   SKILLS

BEHAVIOR|GAP

Without trust, there is no true relationship. Does the advisor show trustworthiness? Do they look you in the eye? Is the advisor doing all the talking? Are they talking to you or talking *down* to you? Do they call when they say they will? Do they do the things they say they will do? Ask yourself "Do I genuinely like this person?" Would you be friends with this person? Do you feel comfortable with them? Are they telling you hard truths or just sugar-coating, saying that everything is wonderful? Do they hold you account-able? Do you feel that the advisor likes you? Or do you get the feeling the advisor *doesn't* like *you* as a person—obviously that's a red flag. You are about to enter into an intimate relationship that will hopefully last a long time. If you have any reservations with this, move on. There are plenty of qualified advisors out there who would like to help you.

Here are a few things that you should observe about the advisor. They are consistent, and you can depend on them because they:

- Don't substitute their judgment for yours

- Help you to think and separate your logic from your emotions

- Don't pull their punches (you can rely on them to tell you the truth)

- Give you reasoning (help you to think), not just their conclusions

- Challenge your assumptions (help you to uncover the false assumptions under which you've been working)

- Make you feel comfortable and casual personally (but they take the issues seriously)

- Act like a real person, not someone in a role

- Are reliably on your side and always seem to have your interests at heart

- Have a sense of humor to diffuse (your) tension in tough situations[11]

---

11 www.fool.com/investing/general/2016/05/21/5-signs-you-can-trust-your-financial-advisor.aspx

Other things that are important to think about: Does your advisor talk openly about risk with you? Any advisor who tries to downplay the risks associated with investing is effectively doing wrong by his clients. In addition to talking about risk, he should run numbers showing you what you stand to gain and lose in different market scenarios.

Background Check: How to Check Them Out and What to Look for

"That's why you do your homework. It is important to have all your ducks in a row before you do something"

— *Tim Davis*

"Is there anything in your regulatory record that I should know about?" Actually, you don't even have to ask them about their regulatory record: You can go online and get all this information before you even meet with them. This is the first line of defense. Part of your research should include conducting background checks on the professional you may hire. You can visit the Securities & Exchange Commission (www.sec.gov) and FINRA (www.finra.org) websites or the State Securities website NASAA (www.nasaa.org) as well as the CFP Board at (www.cfp.net). While some violations are nonstarters (settlement of multiple customer complaints), others may be understandable (marketing materials not preapproved; non-client or investment violations).

Check BrokerCheck www.brokercheck.finra.org and look at the advisor's past. If you see 37 lawsuits against the advisor, that might be a clue you should avoid them like the plague. I know you think I am exaggerating here, but I didn't make this number up. I had clients who were dealing with an advisor like this—the advisor was a family member—and needless to say, it wasn't going great. Now, the flip side is the advisor may have a few inquiries on his record, and some of them can be downright bullsham or else easily explained (I go into my own experience with this in Chapter 10). The best thing to do is read into them and you will get an idea of the story unfolding. It is all right there on BrokerCheck.

If they are an RIA (Registered Investment Adviser), visit the SEC's website and check their record there at www.sec.gov. Also check out the North American Securities Administrators Association at www.nasaa.org).

Utilize Social Media

Go through the advisor's social media pages. This is a *must-do,* in my opinion! Talk about an easy way to get to know someone…. Join Facebook, Twitter, Instagram and LinkedIn if you are not on already and "friend" or "follow" the financial advisor's personal page—not just their business page, their personal page. You can tell a lot about a person from their digital footprint—their pictures, their posts, their likes, opinions, hobbies and interests. When you are going for a job interview, a lot of times the employer interviewing you will go through your social media sites to get an idea of you as a person. The same goes for the police or the FBI—when a crime is committed, one of their first steps is checking out the alleged criminal's social media pages to see what they are doing. Usually, this unlocks a wealth of information regarding the perpetrator's state of mind. We live in a society where many people are open books and it's very easy to find this information right at your fingertips with about 15-30 minutes of your time. In this scenario, you are hypothetically the employer hiring the financial advisor, "the employee," to handle your entire retirement life savings. My point is, it's okay to scope out their social media sites in this instance.

If they look intoxicated in nearly every one of their pictures or spews insane political posts or displays an endless parade of duck-face selfies, there could be an underlying problem.

Additional Key Criteria for Functional Retirement Advisors

"HOW DO I KNOW YOU'RE LEGIT?"

I shouldn't have to mention this, but I will. Make sure you are not dealing with a narcissistic personality. A good example is Bernie Madoff. Here's how the Mayo Clinic describes the narcissistic personality:

"Narcissistic personality disorder is a mental disorder in which people have an inflated sense of their own importance, a deep need for admiration and a lack of empathy for others. But behind this mask of ultra-confidence lies a fragile self-esteem that's vulnerable to the slightest criticism."

One of the most insulting and popular questions we get as advisors with new clients is "How do I know you're not another Bernie Madoff?" Listen, this happens a lot less often than the media portrays that it happens—it's been nearly a decade since Bernie Madoff was arrested in 2008 and sentenced to 150 years in prison for the most infamous $65 billion Ponzi scheme ever. Alerted by his sons, federal authorities arrested Madoff, and he pled guilty to 11 federal crimes and admitted to operating the largest private Ponzi scheme in history with restitution of $170 billion.

What is shocking to note is that Madoff was a *fiduciary*! He was a stockbroker for most of his career—a position that does not require a fiduciary duty—but when he registered as an investment advisor in 2006, he took on a fiduciary duty to his clients. Madoff is the poster child to illustrate that fiduciary status doesn't guarantee honesty. At the end of the day, fiduciary status cannot guarantee any level of competence. Operating under this higher standard does make an advisor more accountable and is something an investor should ask about as part of their screening process; just don't rely on it as the only requirement for an advisor.

The fiduciary standard is intended to protect you. And at the same time, I know some excellent, skilled advisors who put clients first, but work for firms still operating under the lessor suitability standard (a lessor standard than the best-interest standard advisors are held to) which means even though they are subject to the suitability standard, these advisors I know are still doing the right thing. No investment (other than an outright scam) is inherently suitable or unsuitable; it depends on the investor's situation. For example, for a 95-year-old widow living on a fixed income, speculative investments such as options and futures, penny stocks, etc. are extremely unsuitable because the widow has a low risk tolerance. On the other hand, an executive with significant net worth and investing experience might be comfortable taking on those speculative investments as part of his/her portfolio.

While likely none are as big as Madoff's $65 billion fraud, there could still be hundreds of similar schemes in operation across the country. In 2016 alone, 59 schemes were uncovered in the U.S., with alleged losses totaling $2.37 billion, according to data compiled by website Ponzitracker[12] www.ponzitracker.com. Jordan Maglich, the site's creator, said the data shows the unearthing of Ponzi schemes has stayed reasonably consistent over the last five years, both in terms of discoveries and the sentencing of perpetrators.

So while you don't want to be paranoid like the media wants you to be, you obviously don't want to insult your advisor, either. You could ask, "Do you have a financial

---

12 www.ponzitracker.com

interest in the entity that houses my account?" (I call this your Madoff prevention question.) Or you could say, "Where are my funds going to be held? Who is the custodian? Do you have ownership in that custodial firm?" When interviewing advisors not associated with large brokerage or insurance companies, ask if they use an independent, third-party custodian or clearing firm (this is the entity that produces your statements), which prevents the advisor from having direct custody of your assets and adds another level of security for your account. In the Madoff example, he was the investment adviser, broker-dealer, clearing agent and custodian for all of his client accounts. Was sentenced to prison for life.

Let me share a phone conversation that a friend of mine had with a "narcissistic" personality (her advisor). She said that her advisor called and said politely, "How are you doing?" But when she started to answer, she was cut off after about one sentence. She said to me that this was especially offensive to her, because her answer was "I was in a serious car accident and cannot walk." Instead of the advisor asking how she was or at least showing some sympathy, he launched into, essentially, "Me, me, me…me, me, me…, okay, I'm back… me, me… me… I… I… me." Needless to say, she "fired" the advisor.[13]

The hallmark of the narcissist is that once they are in a dominant position over you (i.e., you have hired them), everything is all about them and their needs, to the point of disrespectfulness or absurd clownishness. Here are two

---

13 www.bellatrixlaw.com/you-should-fire-narcissitic-clients-and-customers/

reasons why you should "fire" your advisor if you suspect they may be narcissistic.

1. They will waste your time. A narcissist cares only about themselves, and this means they will not respect your time. They will demand you be available whenever they want, regardless of your schedule.

2. They tend to be drama queens/kings. They do not get along well with lots of people. They may also cheat, steal, scheme, rant, blame, manipulate and cry. A narcissistic advisor will not hesitate to call 15 times in a day or complain about how unfairly they are being paid and say that they are not charging enough for their services.[14]

Are they promising you too high returns? The 10-year treasury bill is 2.8% as of this writing. That means that if you loaned money to the U.S. Government for 10 years, they would give you interest of 2.8% a year. That means things that are said to be *guaranteed* at rates way higher than this are either super-risky or downright questionable—for instance, Bernie Madoff was guaranteeing his clients 16%. Most people are aware of this, but these charlatans prey on an individual's greed.

---

14 www.bellatrixlaw.com/you-should-fire-narcissitic-clients-and-customers/

More Red Flags

"As we gain confidence in ourselves, they are no longer red flags. They are deal breakers."

— Unknown

You've just started working with your new advisor, and they started talking about products first. This is a big red flag. Of course, you may need some products, but not before the creation of a *plan*. Let me point out that the plan doesn't have to be a laborious process, but your advisor must have some sort of plan and understand you as a person. A plan is not a lock or a sure thing, but you <u>may</u> succeed with a plan. Always having something or someone guiding you helps tremendously. Without a plan, you are almost surely not going to succeed financially.

Here are a few more red flags to watch for:

- Your advisor has no significant experience—one to five years' experience is limited time.

- They say they can time the market!

- They tout performance.

- They brag about how much money they make for their clients.

- They have no empathy. All they do is talk, talk, talk.

- They discuss get-rich-quick schemes.

- They talk you into using margin to borrow on your portfolio in order to get higher returns.

Yet Even More Red Flags

- They promise huge returns. Shady "experts" will convince you they've got the winning formula to make you a 10% profit year in, year out.

- They can't explain their strategy simply. They are trying to hide something, whether it's poor choices or hidden fees. And be wary of advisors who say too little: This is also a sign they could be hiding something.

  Jargon, Jargon, Jargon. "Don't worry, we've diversified your investments. You have an average standard deviation in this portfolio so we can push through headwinds and get us some high alpha this year." Huh? If they can't explain their strategy to you in the good times without using jargon, how are they going to communicate with you in a way that brings you comfort during times of financial stress?

- They ignore your spouse or partner. Any advisor worth their salt should be upfront that they serve the interests of both spouses equally.[15]

- You are single and would like your children or a friend to attend the meeting, but your advisor says no. A functional retirement advisor would embrace this.

---

15 www.highya.com/articles-guides/6-red-flags-how-to-find-a-financial-advisor-you-can-really-trust

Succession

Yes, you should have the conversation with your potential advisor about what their legacy plan is should said advisor retire or predecease you, but this is not a make-or-break point in vetting your FRA. While a succession plan is important and shows great responsibility on their part, you don't need to know your advisor's successor from the start. In the event your FRA happens to go under a bus, *then* it's time to pull out this book to hire your future FRA, whether it be their successor or someone from an entirely new firm.

In other words....Go with your gut!

You simply scan them for trust and empathy yourself. Use this book to learn what to look for, and then go and see if you like them as people. It's difficult to vet trust and empathy—this is something you will experience and learn through interaction with that person. But ask yourself these two questions: *Do you like them?* And *do you feel they like you?*

"The only real valuable thing is intuition."

— Albert Einstein

CHAPTER 9

EMPATHY AND QUALITATIVE DATA

"Empathy is seeing with the eyes of another, listening with the ears of another, and feeling with the heart of another."

— Alfred Adler

BEHAVIOR GAP

Does the financial advisor show signs of empathy? How can you tell—do they listen to you? Do they take the time to hear you? I mean HEAR you. Really hear you. Are they trying to understand you? Are they asking questions or just talking *at* you? Do they ask about your family? Do they show signs that they care enough to know you as a person? Do they spend time with you? You ever go to the doctor and always feel like it's a rush? Yeah, you don't want that. You want someone who is going to take their time with you.

As a client, you may be thinking this: "Show me how much you care before you show me how much you know."

A few years back, I learned of an embarrassing example of a dysfunctional financial advisor lacking empathy. I had a couple who had half their money with me and the remainder with another advisor. Unfortunately, the husband suddenly passed away from a heart attack after bravely saving his son and his friend from a riptide. Soon after the funeral, the widow came to me to figure out the family's finances. But the meeting took a turn I wasn't expecting—through her grief, she started to vent about how the other financial advisor took it upon himself to treat her hero husband's wake like a networking opportunity and passed his business cards around to the crowd! Talk about red flags.

Another way of showing empathy, which ties in with the empathy criteria mentioned above, is the QUALitative data criteria. The word "QUALitative" sounds like jargon, but it's not. Let's talk a little more about the "personal" aspects of what QUALitative actually means in plain English.

Personal/Qualitative Data

"To write prescriptions for people is easy, but to come to an understanding with people is hard."

—Franz Kalfka

It is my belief and my own experience that this element is a *critical* one for a Functional Retirement Advisor to possess. This will prove that your "best interests" are being put first. In addition, if the advisor already demonstrates the other four FRA criteria and now wants to know how it all fits in your life, this puts a bright *fiduciary* light on them. Feel out if they have a system for getting the QUALitative/personal data from you.

Here are a few issues you should consider. Do they know how you feel about money? Do they know your deep desires on what to do with this money or why you are saving it in the first place? Do they know your vision and help you come up with this vision? (A vision will help guide the financial plan and give actual, real meaning to your intentions behind this whole thing.) So, just who are you? What is your risk tolerance? How old are you? Retiring? When? Are your parents still living? Will you be their caregiver? What are your assets? How much do you need, both now and in retirement? Most advisors are very good at getting the QUANtitative data from you to help formulate your plan. The QUALitative data, not so much. Your advisor needs both sets of data before they can create the optimal plan that's right for you.

Basically, it's *the why* behind why you and the advisor are doing all of this. Without a *why*, the plan is fragmented and rudderless. Do you even know *why* you are doing this financial planning? What is your true *why*? Does the advisor's process help you to discover that? Does he ask you how you feel about your investments or about your mutual fund or other products? It does not have to be specifically the questions and exercises I ask in this book, but your advisor should have a process (though they may be hesitant to ask you, given some clients' feedback when these types of questions are asked of them). In my experience, sometimes an advisor (and this has happened to me many times) will bring up these types of processes to uncover the client's true goals and aspirations, and the client wants to only deal in the QUANtitative—the numbers, the money. That can work and it has worked, but a much more fulfilling, congruent, satisfying relationship for both the client and the advisor happens when you also have the QUALitative information.

I'm hoping this book opens the minds of clients and helps them to realize that it's best to open up with their advisor on their true heart's desires. So, if the advisor meets all the other criteria mentioned here and you like them and trust them, this is one of the pieces I can help you to help them with. Looking at George Kinder's three questions in this book on page 15 and then presenting your answers to the advisor that you may already trust is a *fantastic* way to gauge their empathy and look for signs that they care for you as a person. I suggest this exercise of answering these types of questions and bringing them to the advisor that you trust, and who has the other criteria for being an FRA, and you can do this without them even having to ask. This would tell you everything you need to know about the criteria of empathy—which is them caring enough to know you as a person. This would be the closest thing to a person who is in a vulnerable position to have this advisor see you as a person and not just some "sale." They will know what makes you tick and gear the whole plan and the decisions along the way around this information—if they are of value, that is. It is the closest thing to you (the client) having the financial education yourself when the advisor knows you this intimately. The QUALitative data ties in with how to know if they have empathy.

But what about getting to know the advisor as a person? You are trusting this person with your entire financial life, so it would be greatly beneficial for you to learn the advisor's story—who they are, what challenges they may have faced and how they overcame them.

Here's a little bit of my story. After graduation from St. John's University, I started my financial planning career at Merrill Lynch in New York City. After two grueling years in Merrill's training program, I managed to build up a decent practice in a few years. Meanwhile, Wachovia had been courting me, and once they sweetened the deal to the point that I could no longer resist by offering me bank branches that would refer clients to me, I decided to make the move to New Jersey. One problem—when I first got hired by Merrill Lynch, I signed a non-compete clause which stated that I was not able to contact or solicit clients once I left the firm. That meant leaving behind six years' worth of work without a moment's notice to my clientele. In my naivety, I thought (hoped) my Merrill clients would somehow find me across the river, but that fantasy evaporated real quick and I was left to restart my business from scratch. The odds are stacked against you to build up a financial planning practice one time, let alone twice, but here I was. Throw on top of that a divorce, and I was on the edge of Nervous Breakdown City. However, I held it together, stuck to the same principles that helped me succeed at Merrill (but armed with infinitely more experience) and built up my practice again.

Three short years later, that moral victory turned out to be short-lived, however, when the 2008 stock market came crashing down on me and everyone in the industry like a ton of bricks. To make matters even more unsettled, Wachovia was taken over by Wells Fargo, and with that came an entirely new financial advisor program that I was not keen on. No longer wanting to be beholden to the "Big Boys," I decided to take my biggest risk to date and start an independent practice—only this time, I was going to figure out how to make sure my clients came with me...legally, of course. I hired an attorney and placed tombstone ads (basic newspaper announcements) in the local papers saying where I was going and how I could be reached. Most, if not all, of my clients followed me. Today I enjoy a mutually beneficial relationship with a lot of those same people (and more), as well as the freedom and flexibility that comes with being your own boss. However, those humbling lessons I learned early on are never far from my mind, and they have taught me to treat everyone—in and out of business—with compassion and understanding.

I tell this story to all potential clients that ask me—and I'm telling it to you—because I feel it is important to know the advisor as a person, both personally and professionally. I am not saying you have to be best friends, but what I am saying is have the conversation.

CHAPTER 10

HOW MUCH EXPERIENCE IS ENOUGH?

"Experience is the teacher of all things."

-Julius Caesar

"One way of looking at this might be that for 42 years, I've been making small, regular deposits in this bank of experience, education and training. And on January 15, the balance was sufficient so that I could make a very large withdrawal."

- Captain Sully Sullenberger

The required experience of a Functional Retirement Advisor does not include work in another part of the financial world such as trading, compliance, or in management. This experience is not working for a company and dealing on the institutional side of the financial business. This is not someone who ran or worked for a hedge fund, nor is it someone who represented a mutual fund, nor is it someone who worked on the floor of a stock exchange. I hear advisors say they've been in this business for 20 years, but 10 to 15 of those years were in a different capacity in the financial world. Or they were a lawyer or an accountant for 15 years and now all of a sudden they've been in the financial-planning business for the last five years. Or they have a full time job and do retirement planning on occasion. You can't live and breathe this stuff while doing another stressful time-consuming job. That's called multi-careering. I don't want my retirement future with people who are not 100% "all in." Now, if they multi-career and have a Functional Retirement Advisor on their team, that's another story. That could be optimal, such as if a CPA who is a planner also has an FRA on his team.

I'm talking 15 years minimum of blood, sweat and tears in the financial-planning world with individuals. It is that simple. Why am I drilling this into your skull?

I see this a lot, as if that's all the same experience rolled into one, which couldn't be farther from the truth.

I toyed with the idea of making it 20 years minimum, because as of this writing you would be standing in front of an advisor who has been in the financial-planning business helping individuals who have been through two major bear markets: 2001–2002 and 2008–2009. Right now if you are working with an advisor that has been doing individual financial planning for eight years or less, they have only *read* about bear markets. They do not have the important ingredient of helping people through these difficult times. They aren't truly tested yet. Fifteen to twenty years' experience (ongoing) gives you one, or even two large financial draw-downs, which gives your advisor hard-core experience. Ask your advisor about these times and how he handled them. What got him and his clients through them? (As a side note: I would think about your own personal investment experience in the 2008–2009 downturn of the markets. What did you do with your investments during that time? How did you react? How did you feel?)

The only way to learn anything in this world is to experience it. You want someone who has helped individuals in retirement, through retirement and in all the other life transitions. People go through all different sorts of stages in life, like divorce, grandchildren, retirement, downsizing their home, long-term care, marriage, relocation, loss of a spouse, second marriage, and/or illness as we age. You don't want advisors practicing on you. In addition to life transitions, there are also all different types of market/economic cycles, market crashes, market panics, market booms, and market euphorias.

I equate it to flying: You want a pilot with major experience under their belt in case of an in-flight emergency. Look at Sully Sullenberger, the United Airways captain who skillfully and calmly navigated his Airbus A320 to land on the Hudson River after a flock of Canadian geese struck his engines. If there was a less experienced pilot at the helm, the fate of all 155 souls on board would have been tragically different on that January 15, 2009.

I'm not saying what an FRA does is life-or-death like in that instance, but when the going gets tough, don't you want that same veteran poise to help you through critical lifetime changes and market catastrophes?

Fifteen years is a good barometer for an advisor going through enough economic market cycles and should have helped enough clients for long enough to go through the life transitions mentioned. Think about this: You don't want mistakes made because of inexperience when you are dealing with crucial retirement monies at or near retirement. Mistakes get made, and with your retirement, when you very possibly have the most money you will ever have in your life, it is not the time to leave your life savings and retirement success to chance with inexperience.

As an example, when I first began in the financial services industry at Merrill Lynch as a financial advisor, I went through the company's rigorous financial advisor training program for two years. This was around 1999 or 2000, when everyone was coming in asking, indeed *begging*, to sell out of their perfectly diversified portfolios to put everything they had, or big portions of it, into high-rising tech stocks that were doubling, tripling, etc. This is the epitome of a market cycle where "greed" sets in and investors cannot control their emotions. But—are you able to handle a downturn? Are you prepared for that?

At that time, as a young advisor at Merrill Lynch, we were told to counsel clients into sticking with their portfolios. Many listened, some did not. But as tech stocks continued to skyrocket, Merrill started to become intoxicated by the fad and developed its own Global Tech Fund. Being a good soldier to Mother Merrill, I decided to talk some of my clients into investing into a portion of this fund. In one instance, I put my client in an UTMA/UGMA (Uniform Gift to Minors Act) account for his son. Thankfully, it wasn't a large amount; I was at least smart enough to do small numbers!

When the dot.com bubble burst, the fund was down 50% to 70%. While this was only a portion of the portfolio—and while the clients knew the risks—getting them into this fund in the first place was a rookie mistake. I shouldn't have bought into the media/friends/family/client overhype, but it was a result of my not being through enough market cycles.

This situation actually wound up being a pesky mark on my license. When my client's son turned 18 years old and came into the money from this UTMA account, he accused me of doing an unauthorized trade with his father, meaning that I acted without the son's knowledge. However, at the time he was a minor, and his father had the authority over the account and knew full well about the trade. Merrill came to my defense and explained that the son's complaint had no merit and was completely ludicrous, everyone (besides the son) was in full agreement, but according to FINRA rules, it must be disclosed. This is why, as I mentioned earlier in this book, it's important to do your homework on your potential FRA. If they have any sort of disclosure on their record, it's important to read and understand them on BrokerCheck.com.

CHAPTER 11

THE ADVISOR'S FINANCIAL STABILITY— IT'S OKAY TO ASK

"When we see a man with bad shoes, we say it is no wonder, if he is a shoemaker."

- Michel de Montaigne

This is a BIG one. I don't understand how the regulators miss this one. I learned this from working at the bank as a financial advisor for long enough. In my opinion, most of the time things are done incongruently because the advisor is desperate to make the sale either to pay for their own expenses, indulgences or to meet the sales goals set by their firm. Here's the thing: They may drive a Ferrari or another luxury car, wear a Rolex watch or have a gorgeous solid-oak finished office with leather furniture. Don't be fooled: This can all be window dressing and does not mean they are financially stable. They may be *all flash* and *no cash*. I am not saying there is anything wrong with having nice things (who doesn't like nice things?), but just make sure they are also practicing what they preach.

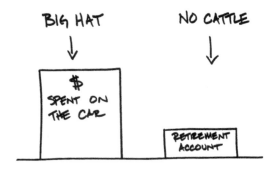

Ask your advisor about their finances, ask them their net worth, ask if they would share with you their financial plan, how much they have invested, what their plan and goals look like. They're asking *you,* aren't they? I believe it is very important to know that your advisor is financially solvent.

If they are just starting out and they don't have the assets yet, that's fine—as long as they are not spending more than they take in every month. However, let's not forget to vet the 15 year experience criteria. I do not have any specific numbers in mind that must be met by the advisor's net worth; just simply have the conversation and your gut will tell you all you need to know.

An added bonus is when the advisor shows you their financial plan and they explain that they have another advisor helping them with their own financial plan. This would show that the advisor is smart enough to know that even an FRA needs an FRA! That is how emotional money can be, and remember, advisors' money is tied to their emotions, too. (They don't *have* to be working with an advisor—just saying, that would count for extra points if they indeed are.)

Know that when you are dealing with an advisor who is not somewhat financially okay that some of the recommendations they make for you may or may not be in your best interest. This is not one-size-fits-all, but I think it should be a prerequisite to dealing with people's money. As for the younger, less experienced advisors with fewer assets, I believe they should be on teams of advisors who are financially sound. If they are on such a team, that means they may be compensated for helping the senior advisor as well as running their own clientele. Hopefully, this would help the young advisor not to be in a financial quagmire themselves. The same goes for advisors with less than 15-plus years of experience as well; they should be on a team with an experienced advisor on whom they can bounce ideas off.

Bring an NDA (nondisclosure form) to your FRA to make him feel comfortable that you will not tell anyone else his private financial information. (See sample in Appendix.) I would say you want an FRA who is financially successful, is saving enough money each year and has a written financial plan using the financial-planning software program they are telling you to use. I can't tell you how many advisors don't have their own financial plan. This is not to say the advisor is dishonest. All I'm saying is that the financially sound ones are *a lot* less likely to do things for their benefit over yours. One bank rep I worked with used to do all his transactions based on how much money he made. This is not the norm, but there are reps like this, and the reason was that he was having a hard time paying his own bills. That's what I call a bona fide dysfunctional advisor. Another one said that he has to earn high commissions every month to support his "expensive" family—this after telling me how much he spends on motorcycles, cars and a second beach home.

During my 22 years in the business, I remember one particularly egregious case. An advisor I knew was actually paying his mortgage out of a few of his clients' accounts. We were all completely surprised he was doing this, and how he was able to do that, I have no idea! But the fact remains that he was doing that, and one day the Feds came in and busted him. That was more than 10 years ago, and he is probably still in jail. My point is you don't want to be with a desperado. Unfortunately, since this is a "sales"/ non-salaried business much of the time, there are a decent number of advisors who are not financially sound, and that does increase the odds of their doing things for their own interest and benefit first.

Most people blindly go with an advisor and do not ask them about their financial situation. You can't blame them—most people get on an airplane without even so much as looking at the pilot.

I am not saying you must be working with an advisor that is a multimillionaire, but making sure they are at least in the black every year and that they have a decent amount of money stored away for their age group is a good rule of thumb. This just stacks the deck in your favor. This is all your call; the guidelines I pointed out in this book give you a greater chance of getting a fiduciary. It doesn't indicate that the advisors who are not reaching all five of these guideposts in this book are necessarily bad people or bad advisors. I am just saying the chances of you getting a true fiduciary goes up exponentially, in my opinion, when the advisor has all of these characteristics.

Let's remember what you are betting on this. It is your life savings that has to pay your cost of living from the day you retire to the day you and your spouse (if you are married) die. And you definitely want some assets left over for your children or heirs. Let's not forget what we are up against (re-read Chapter 3 on 21st-century retirement if needed). You are swapping your paycheck for a check that comes from your investments in retirement.

People are going to say, just because the advisor has money, can't they be greedy and looking out for their own piece of the pie? Yes, of course that could be the case. That is why financial stability is not the only criteria. The FRA must have trust, empathy, QUALitative data, 15 plus years of experience, CFP®, ChFC, practices investor behavioral management AND financial stability. They can be financially stable, but still not trustworthy, nor show empathy, nor care about you as a person. You have to look at the whole picture; the FRA must be sound in all five of the criteria.

CHAPTER 12

ALPHABET SOUP CAN BE IMPORTANT

Let's talk a bit about some of the accreditations and what they mean to you and to your advisors.

AIF®: Accredited Investment Fiduciary means they should have a system in place for all sorts of fiduciary rules. The advisor knows the checks and balances and should be implementing them. An example is the IPS—the Investment Policy Statement. For your managed accounts, there should be an IPS, which is the business plan for the investments. It gives you the parameters you agreed to for your investments. It is what kind of investments according to what you need in return to get to your goals, as well as what kind of downside risk and range of returns there should be. Your AIF-accredited advisor has a duty to monitor the investments. Most of the brokerage firms have already leveled the commissions on some products to lesson advisors using them for big profits.

CFP®: Certified Financial Planner. Your advisor should have a good accreditation like the CFP, which is known as the gold standard in the financial-planning arena. The CFP is a great program. It is a rigorous study period with a rigorous test to pass, and it requires continuing education on estate tax, investments, taxes, retirement planning, insurance and so on. CFPs need to earn 30 credits every two years, which is enough for them to understand all the changes that take place. There are other accreditations that are okay and some that are bull sham. But this one is perfect for what we are looking for. Yes, yes, yes the CFA® (Certified Financial Analyst) is a harder, more excruciating test than even the CFP, however it's good for a stock picker

A CFP *must* tell you about their conflicts of interest. You need to know what else the advisor is getting paid for. Most of the time it shouldn't be an issue that they get paid on other pieces of business. If they are doing a good job and doing it all holistically this will, and should, be the case, in my opinion. However, like the CFP Board, I want you to know and the CFP standard is they MUST tell you these conflicts of interest.

More good news about a CFP. They are automatically signed up to act as a fiduciary, so you don't have to ask them to sign a form about it. This is easier for you and for them.

ChFC®: Chartered Financial Consultant. The ChFC® designation has been a mark of excellence for financial planners for almost 30 years, and it currently requires more courses than any other financial-planning credential. The curriculum covers extensive education and application training in all aspects of financial planning, income taxation, investments, and estate and retirement planning. Continuing Education: It requires 30 hours of continuing education every two years. Accreditation: The American College has the highest level of educational accreditation—regional accreditation—through the Middle States Commission on Higher Education.

The big difference between the ChFC and the CFP: The CFP has a very rigorous test that advisors must pass; the ChFC does not.

CIMA®: Certified Investment Management Analyst. The Investment Management Consultants Association (IMCA) grants the CIMA designation, which is designed specifically for financial professionals who want to attain a level of competency as an advanced investment consultant. The educational component is offered through the Wharton School at the University of Pennsylvania. Topics include modern portfolio theory, asset allocation, manager search and selection, investment policy and performance measurements. Candidates must pass a Qualification Examination prior to enrolling in the education program and undergo a background check through IMCA. The CIMA credential is accredited by the American National Standards Institute. IMCA was recently rebranded to the Investments & Wealth Institute.

CFA®: Chartered Financial Analyst. CFA is a professional designation given by the CFA Institute that measures the competence and integrity of financial analysts. Candidates are required to pass three levels of exams covering areas such as accounting, economics, ethics, money management and security analysis. CFA program entrants must have a bachelor's or equivalent degree or have four years of qualified professional work experience. The CFA charter is one of the most respected designations in finance, and it is considered by many to be the gold standard in the field of investment analysis.

RIA: Registered Investment Adviser. An RIA is an adviser or firm engaged in the investment advisory business and registered with either the Securities and Exchange Commission (SEC) or state securities authorities. They are financial fiduciaries.

IAR: Investment Adviser Representative. This is a financial fiduciary who works for an investment advisory company whose main responsibility is to provide investment-related advice. According to regulations, IARs can only provide advice on topics on which they have passed the appropriate examinations. They must also be registered with the proper state authorities.

Wealth Manager: A high-level professional who combines financial and investment advice, accounting and tax services, retirement planning, and legal or estate planning for one set fee. Some wealth managers also provide banking services or advice on philanthropic activities.

Stockbroker: Also called a Registered Representative, this professional executes buy and sell orders for stocks and other securities through a stock market or over the counter for a fee or commission. He or she may work for a stock-brokerage firm.

Remember, some of these letters and designations after the advisor's name mean that, technically, they have already agreed to be fiduciaries. This is a good thing, but it means that if things go wrong, you have the right to go after them with a lawsuit—UGLY. When they have all of the other FRA criteria I describe in this book in addition to, let's say, the CFP designation, it means we are being more proactive in our research of the advisor *beforehand.* Meaning...*prevention.*

Source: http://www.designationcheck.com/

CHAPTER 13

BEHAVIORAL MANAGEMENT / INVESTING

"The way I see it, if you want the rainbow, you gotta put up with the rain."

— Dolly Parton

FACTORS THAT DRIVE RETURNS

1- BEHAVIOR
2- % IN STOCKS
3- % IN SMALL STOCKS
4- % IN VALUE STOCKS

*MARKET TIMING, STOCK
PICKING, CNBC, YOUR
BROTHER-IN-LAW...

BEHAVIOR|GAP

Behavioral Investment Management should be part of your criteria for choosing a Functional Retirement Advisor. Your FRA does not stop at standard discussions about your financial goals and investments. Behavioral Investment Management incorporates the science of stress and decisions along with your life event experiences to help you lower your anxiety, evaluate more choices, feel confident in your decisions and enjoy what you've worked so hard to build.

I have learned the importance of Behavioral Management through my 22 years of experience in this business, coupled with the teachings of my mentor, Nick Murray. Nick has been a financial advisory professional for more than 50 years. He is one of the financial industry's premier speakers and the author of 12 books for financial service professionals. His one book for clients, *Simple Wealth Inevitable Wealth*, is a fantastic read for individuals to understand principles for building prosperity over time. I highly recommend clients to read it. I had seen him speak at a Merrill Lynch conference back in the early 2000's and was struck by how he was able to eloquently boil down complicated topics such as retirement and investing to simple, easy to understand truths. I started to read all of his books and became a subscriber of his monthly newsletter and every year I attend his annual Behavior Investment Conference in New York City where approximately 200 outstanding financial advisors, from across the country, and I learn the importance, the basics and critical emotions of how to help our clients to work "through" markets rather than "to" markets.

Lessons of Investment Behavioral Management

"Optimism is the only realism. It is the only worldview which squares with the facts, and with the historical record."

— Nick Murray, Simple Wealth,
Inevitable Wealth

Practicing behavior management and behavior investing with your FRA in respect to your retirement nest egg is crucial. This is important because poor past performance is what worries people—like bear markets, of course. For portfolio growth during your retired life, you have to consider putting a portion of your retirement savings in equities (stock).

A long-term, quality, diversified portfolio of equities should be an absolute for at least the long-term money of retirement. The amount of how much of your personal portfolio should be earmarked for this is a whole discussion you must have with your FRA. An unwritten rule of what qualifies for long-term money in retirement is any money that you do not need to use for anywhere between 5-10 years and beyond. Let's not forget how long retirement is going to be—20 to 30 years of your living in retirement. Some people get nervous with the sheer mention of equities in retirement. Many investors do not understand that when they are investing in stocks, they are investing in *companies.* You are owning a piece of this company. In a diversified portfolio, that's small pieces of *many* companies. Yes, there will be times when your diversified portfolio is down, but because of the planning you did with your FRA, it should be money you won't need at that time, so you can withstand the downturn. In the 21st-century retirement, to overcome everything we're up against as well as to get our wants, needs and goals we have to guard our purchasing power over time and realize that we can't just define risk as losing part of our principal.

Most people don't realize that a big part of retirement risk in the 21st-century retirement is outliving one's money. There must be a part of the retirement plan that includes a diversified, quality equity portfolio for growth of *income* and your *principal* throughout your retirement years. You just have to sit down and have a discussion with your FRA for a blueprint about this as well as stomaching the downturns, which WILL happen.

Bear Markets

*"Among the four most dangerous words in investing:
It's different this time"*

—Sir John Templeton

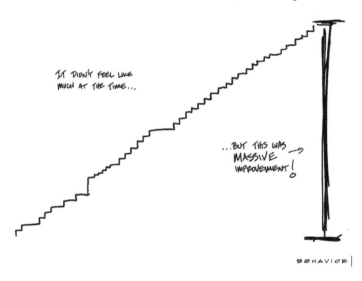

IT DIDN'T FEEL LIKE MUCH AT THE TIME...

...BUT THIS WAS MASSIVE IMPROVEMENT!

BEHAVIOR

Let's talk a bit about bear markets now. Since WWII, there have been 14 bear markets. This averages out to be one every five years or so. There are many different ways to define a bear market, but I am defining a bear market as a decline in equity prices of 20% or more. How we react to these bear markets will determine how well we will do in the 21st-century retirement. It is critical to understand this to have a functional retirement. It is equally important to understand that you need a Functional Retirement Advisor to guide you through these markets properly and to make sure that you are prepared before they hit. This is all with a plan based on your individual situation to help guide both you and the FRA.

Dates of Market Peak	Dates of Market Trough	% Return	Duration	Market Peak	Market Trough
05/29/46	06/13/49	-30%	36.5 Months	19.3	13.6
08/02/56	10/22/57	-22	14.5 Months	49.7	39.0
12/12/61	06/26/62	-28	6.5 Months	72.6	52.3
02/09/66	10/07/66	-22	8.0 Months	94.1	73.2
11/29/68	05/26/70	-36	18.0 Months	108.4	69.3
01/11/73	10/03/74	-48	20.5 Months	120.2	62.3
09/21/76	03/06/78	-19	17.5 Months	107.8	86.9
11/28/80	08/12/82	-27	20.5 Months	140.5	102.4
08/25/87	12/04/87	-34	4.0 Months	336.8	223.9
07/16/90	10/11/90	-20	3.0 Months	369.0	295.5
07/17/98	08/31/98	-19	1.5 Months	1186.8	957.3
03/24/00	10/09/02	-49	30.5 Months	1527.5	776.7
10/09/07	03/09/09	-57 .	17.0 Months	1565.1	676.5
04/29/11	10/03/11	-19.4	5.0 Months	1363.6	1099.2

Source: Standard & Poor's

Source: Nick Murray's Bear Markets Seminar 2018

Once again, I must stress that this is NOT about timing these bear markets or trying to avoid them. (Nobody can do that consistently.) The fact is they WILL happen. Notice I did not say <u>may</u> happen or <u>can</u> happen. They WILL happen from time to time. One critical piece to a successful retirement lifetime is how you react to these market declines. So let's check out the facts of bear markets along with the feelings—the typical human emotions that pop up during these times (which is very important in order to deal with these inevitable declines). Your FRA is not there to help you with the facts during these critical times, nor to time these 20% or more declines. They are there to help you deal with the feelings. They are there to empathize with you as you feel the fear, and to help you decide not to act on that fear.

You may remember that in 2009 the markets were going down fiercely among tons of chaos for about two years. So, from 2007 to 2009, the market went down anywhere from 30% to 57%. In our lifetime and my career, I had never seen such a drop. Years 2001 and 2002 were bad, but not as bad as 2007 to 2009. The media kicked it up a notch. Screaming on TV, in the newspapers, on the internet that IT IS ALL OVER!!!! People were coming in to my office, calling very concerned about their monies and telling me that their friends got out of the market. My clients had well-diversified portfolios, with a financial plan and we had discussed not getting out of the markets. Clients would say, "Joe, we really like you, you are a great guy, we trust you, but these investments aren't working out. You told us to stick it out and we did, and so far all it does is keep going down—we want to get out, all of our friends are getting out or have gotten out." I would reply, "That's a big mistake. I don't know how or why, but at some point it will come back. Don't make that mistake." Most of the clients stayed with it. The S&P 500 (Standard & Poor's 500), an American stock market index based on the market capitalization of 500 of the largest companies in the United States, went down and was around 757 points on March 1, 2009. As of January 1, 2018 it is at 2,683. Do you think the clients that stuck to their investment strategy during the downturn were helped to achieve their wants, needs and goals? Do you think they are better off now, especially the ones that are preparing for retirement? Do you think the few who didn't listen or the people that didn't have an FRA are having a hard time now? How do you think their friends fared?

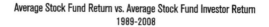

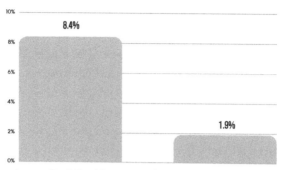

Average Stock Fund Return vs. Average Stock Fund Investor Return 1989-2008

DALBAR, *Inc. is the financial community's leading independent expert for evaluating, auditing and rating business practices, customer performance, product quality and service. They are committed to raising the standards of excellence in the financial services. Since 1994, DALBAR's Quantitative Analysis of Investor Behavior (QAIB) has measured the effects of investor decisions to buy, sell and switch into and out of mutual funds. The results consistently show that the average investor earns less- in many cases much less- than mutual fund performance reports would suggest.*[16] *The above bar graph shows from 1989-2008 the last great crisis.*

As financial advisors, we do planning and investment behavior modification, helping the client differentiate between logic and emotions, and keeping human emotions in check. Nick Murray correctly points out that we, as advisors, don't do economic forecasting, marketing timing or handicapping

---

16 *www.dalbar.com*

of future relative performance based on past performance. We don't start with a product, we start with a PLAN.

FRAs usually don't talk much about, nor have an opinion about, the markets. They are usually asking questions of their clients. Questions such as, what are they going to live on in the 30th year of retirement? Most people may have a tough time keeping up with their cost of living in their retirement because of the conventional wisdom out there that states that you should only be worried about protecting your principle. In reality, it is all about protecting your purchasing power. There are two main retirement questions you should be focusing on: Do you know exactly how much money it is going to take to retire comfortably? And to remain retired comfortably?

Is your advisor telling you that most people do not get market returns? I am happy with market returns over the long run. The market works if you allow it to work. Good companies are rewarded over time. Your advisor should be guiding you to not look at beating markets; it should be about being approximately right rather than being really wrong. It is about having the plan, then using long-term historical numbers to get to the goals in that plan and not being swayed by what's going on in the short term. The FRA provides the courage to stay invested.

The problem with bear markets is that most people forget about them during long bull markets, and they are caught off-guard. This scares them into making mistakes, and then they get out. All the more reason to have the Functional Retirement Advisor by your side the entire time, because it's difficult to handle the emotions without their guidance. This is where I must remind you: Past results are not a guarantee of future returns.

The individual circumstances in each bear market are different enough to scare us half to death, and so-called "experts" on television will tell you with convincing reasons that this time is different. Journalists will also write, "We have never seen anything like this."

(As a side note, if it ACTUALLY happens to be different this time, money will be the least of our problems!)

Let's discuss a few of these bear markets.

2000-2002 bear market: Enron, the accounting scandals, 9/11, recession, looming war in IRAQ.

1998: Russia's default, the "Asian Contasion," the implosion of Long-Term Capital Management, the world's largest hedge fund.

1990-1991: recession, war in the Gulf, the liquidation of the entire savings and loan system in a real estate mess that threatened all banks.

1987: the largest one-day decline in the American equity market, before or since.

1980-1982: Twenty percent interest rates, ten percent unemployment, twelve percent inflation: the horror of stagflation.

All unique! All different! Yet all resolved! Important to note is that when we were going through them, it was impossible to say how they would start and how they would get solved. You did not have to know how they were to start nor how they were to be solved. Indeed no one did. Yet they all were resolved.

Bear markets are caused by economic, financial and even geopolitical problems. The 2008–2009 market is a prime example. It was unique because the global credit system stopped in its tracks after the failure of Freddie Mac, Fannie Mae, Lehman Brothers and AIG—and the global economy fell off a cliff. It felt different this time, and we tried to understand what was happening and how it would end so we could make good informed decisions with our money. AND THERE WAS NOBODY TO TELL US. So we might have felt justified in liquidating our portfolios and going to the safety of "cash."

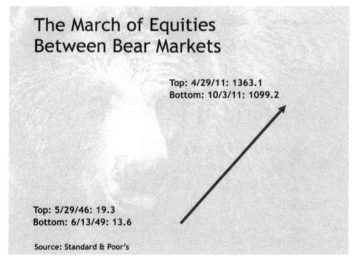

Source: Nick Murray's Bear Markets Seminar 2018

Notice at the bottom of the last bear market, the index was about 80 times higher than the bottom of the first one. Let me point out, that this illustration ignores seven decades of dividends! We are just looking at the price levels of the index in the illustration. These are the kinds of principles and truths to look for in a Functional Retirement Advisor's talk when they meet with you. This is truth. This is simple, but it isn't easy to do.

> *"Don't try to time the market. It's very difficult to do. There may be a couple of people in the world who can do it, but if there are, they're not telling you."*
>
> —Ben Bernanke

> *"....The declines have all been temporary, at least so far and they have been completely overwhelmed by the subsequent advances..."*
>
> — Nick Murray

Volatility Verses Risk

> *"If you can't endure upwards of fifteen percent decline every year, and an average decline of about a third one year in five, you just flat-out can never be an equity investor"*
>
> — Nick Murray

> *"When nothing is sure, everything is possible."*
>
> — Margaret Drabble

"In efficient markets, the suppression of volatility must ultimately result in a commensurate suppression of return."

— Nick Murray

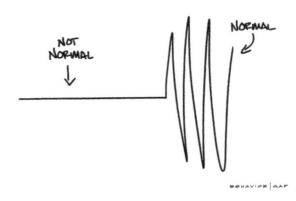

Conventional wisdom from the media will have you thinking the terms volatility and risk are the same thing. However, for the long-term investor they differ in very important ways. I stress that the possible differences between volatility and risk have historically shown up over longer time frames. So one of the ideas I will suggest as you look through the following three graphics is that the effect of volatility on the investor's decision-making depends on the element of time.

Here is a chart provided by Standard & Poor's of the period 1946 through 2017. It shows the frequency of significant price declines in the S&P 500 Stock Index (which was, prior to 1958, the S&P 90, but the math is consistent).

Note these are declines in the price of the index; they ignore the effects of dividends.

A History of Declines
1946-2017

Type of Decline	Total Number of Declines	Average
10% or more	55	Once a year
15% or more	21	Once every 3 years
20% or more	14	Once every 5 years

Source: Standard & Poors

Source: Nick Murray's Volatility Seminar 2018

What you see is that in 72 years there have been 55 intra-year declines of 10% or more. Even more important is the fact that the average intra-year decline in these 72 years was approximately 14%. Please stop and think about that for a moment.

Further, there has been 21 declines of at least 15% or more—that is, an average of one every three years.

And now the big statistic: fourteen declines of at least 20% or more, or one about every five years, and the average of those is closer to 30%. Can you imagine wanting to own an investment whose history, over the last two thirds of a century, was to have you watch an average of 30% of your capital melt away on an average of every six years or so? WHY WOULD ANYONE WANT TO EVER DO THAT?

Well, I can actually think of a couple of reasons. Here, in its most simplistic form, is the big reason.

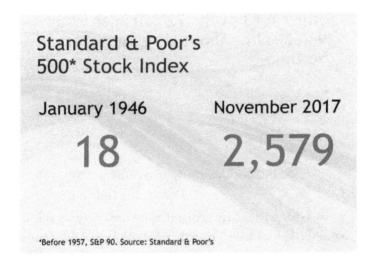

Source: Nick Murray's Volatility Seminar 2018

Yes, that is not a typo, from the beginning of 1946 through November 2017, the Index went from about 18 to well over 2500—even amid all that horrific volatility.

In how many of those 72 years from 1946-2017 would you guess that equities produced a positive return?

53

The S&P 500 has had a positive annual return in 53 of the 72 calendar years 1946-2017 or about three quarters of the time.

Source: Standard & Poor's

Source: Nick Murray's Volatility Seminar 2018

So, what we see here is that despite their very significant volatility, equites have not only produced attractive returns over a long period of time, but they have produced positive returns the great majority of the time—74% of full calendar years. The lesson I believe to be learned from this is that, at least over the particular two thirds of a century we have been looking at, volatility has been defeated by time. Now, I cannot stress enough that as long as potentially credible as these 72 years may have been, THEY DO NOT PROVE ANYTHING. Because when it comes to the future, and especially the future of equities, NOTHING IN THE PAST PROVES ANYTHING ABOUT THE FUTURE.

I have no way to predict the future, much less time the markets, neither can your FRA. But I also do not know how to make investment policy out of chaos theory coming from the media. So I am left to make long-term policy out of what I think is a reasonable probability based on historical experience. And history suggests that the longer our time horizon, the less near-term volatility ends up becoming real long-term risk.

Allow me to give a quick example in figures. To get an average return of the markets (let's just say, for argument's sake, historically 7% or 8% per year), the advisor must be telling you the hard truth that your investment may be down or up at any time, plus or minus 15% to 30%. That means your hypothetical $100k investment can be worth $85k to $70k at any time or up to as high as $125k. Once in a while there will be a big drop that will scare everyone, including me. Remember, it's okay to feel the fear, just don't make rash decisions on it. That goes for your advisor as well.

Let me make this point another way.

At any time on our course to your goals, we are on target sometimes and off target sometimes. This makes me think about the movie *Apollo 13*: The astronauts were set on a path to get from the Earth to the moon in three days. However, the trajectory that they were on was only on target 12 times. Sometimes they were below it, sometimes they were above it…but they still got there.

Your Number

"Appear as you are. Be as you appear."

— Rumi

THE 5 BIG QUESTIONS:
① HOW MUCH CAN YOU SAVE?
② HOW MUCH RISK?
③ HOW MUCH WILL YOU NEED?
④ WHEN WILL YOU NEED IT?
⑤ WHAT DO YOU WANT TO LEAVE?

FUTURE

PRESENT

BEHAVIOR GAP

    This refers to the sum of investment capital you need to have on your retirement date, which will, at some reasonable rate of withdrawal, give you the income you need—in addition to your social security and any fixed pension benefit you may have—to live on in that very first year of retirement. Let's try a basic illustration. The numbers may not be exactly relevant to your situation, but the principle behind the method of calculation should apply to just about everyone. Say you decide that the total pre-tax income you need each month in the first year of retirement is $10,000. And you can rely on social security benefits and, perhaps, a fixed pension benefit from a corporate plan for $4,000 a month. So you will be looking for your investments to be throwing off the other $6,000 ($10,000 in expenses minus $4,000 fixed income from pension and social security) each month for that first year. Please note that I didn't say your investment had to **yield** $6,000, in terms of interest and dividends. I am simply talking about an amount you would be comfortable **withdrawing** each month to support your lifestyle.

Six thousand dollars a month is $72,000 a year. Now we are going to make an assumption, which is that, in order to try and leave your capital intact, and even to give it a chance to keep growing, you will want to withdraw no more than four and a half percent that first year.

So we ask: of what capital sum is $72,000 four and a half percent? And by dividing $72,000 by .045, we arrive at your number. Which is $1,600,000. This is a good exercise to do with your FRA or even before you go to see your FRA. Once you have your number, then you and your FRA can come up with a plan to figure out how much you have now in a retirement investment portfolio, totally apart from other things you may have to pay for, like your children's education. Then your FRA can assess the gap, if any, between where you are right now, and where you need to go to get to your number. This, along with how long you have to close this gap. Using this process you can come to a rough idea of where you are now, where you need to go, and with a conversation with your FRA, figure out how to close this gap in terms of an appropriate portfolio as well as any additions you can make in the years leading up to retirement. From this, you and your FRA can make a fair estimate of what rate of return you are going to need between now and retirement to close the gap, and whether the FRA thinks such a rate of return is realistic. If you both decide it is not realistic, you still can discuss options: retire a bit later than you had planned, start off at a lower income, do part time work in retirement, downsize your house, cut out expenses and things like that. If you are already in retirement, this exercise is still very helpful. The math is the same to get to your number, there just isn't any set retirement date in the future, since you are already retired.

This process gets us to the first year of retirement. In a perfect world, you get to your number and you withdraw at 4.5% your $72,000, or whatever it is for you, in that first year of retirement. Then what?

Well, if history is any guide, and it's the only guide we have, the next year your cost of living goes up. Hence, the challenge of 21st century retirement. Trying to keep our income growing at least at the rate the cost of living is going up, in order to sustain our lifestyle without running through our principal.

How To Calculate Your Number

Fill in your numbers (*note this does not include income taxes)

Monthly Income Needed:	$10,000
minus	
Social Security and Pension:	$4,000
equals	
Investment Withdrawal Needed:	**$6,000**
Monthly Income Needed:	$6,000
X 12 months	
Annual Income Needed:	**$72,000**

What sum of capital will produce $ 72,000 per year at a 4.5% withdrawal rate? (72,000 divided by .045)

Your Number:	**$ 1,600,000**

One Solution for the 21st-Century Retirement

"Patience is the key to joy"

— Rumi

"If you think the market's "too high" wait until you see it 20 years from now."

— Nick Murray

The solution discussed here depends on your individual circumstances and how much you allocate to equities (stocks) and bonds/cash. It also depends on how long you can put this money away and how much risk and volatility you can withstand individually in order to put part of your diversified retirement portfolio in equities (stocks). This can and should be determined and *planned* out with your FRA. With all that being said, this simple picture gives you the challenge that everything we buy goes up in price over time.

1987   *2017*

Source: Nick Murray's Retirement-Income Seminar 2018

A postage stamp represents an example (for illustration purposes) of the cost of goods 30 years ago. In 1987, a stamp was 22 cents. The S&P 500 (Standard & Poor's 500), representing investments in the largest companies in the United States, was at 247 on December 31, 1987. In 2017, the stamp has gone up to a cost of 49 cents.

	1987	2017	Retirement of 30 years
The cost of a postage stamp			Increased 2.27 times
The S&P 500 Index	249 12/31/1987	2,579 11/1/2017	Increased 10.44 times

Source: Nick Murray's Retirement-Income Seminar 2018

On November 1, 2017, the S&P 500 had gone up to a price of 2,579. The example above shows that the stamp price has increased roughly 2.27 times in an average retired life of 30 years, and the S&P has gone up roughly 10.44 times in an average retired life of 30 years. As you can see, the S&P Index has outpaced the cost of the stamp over the same time period. We have to know what the problem is before we come up with the solution. Most people, because of conventional wisdom and what we have learned from our parents and grandparents, are working on the wrong problem. They think retirement is a *principal amount of money* problem. Retirement is an *income* problem. Once you swap out your paycheck for your savings check, you will realize this. To buy the goods and services, you will need *income,* and if long-term history is any guide, you will need an income that goes up.

All of our life experience has shown us the problem— the stamp (representing the cost of goods) —as well as the solution: the S&P 500 (representing investments in a diversified portfolio of the great companies of America and the world). I must point out this doesn't mean you only invest in the S&P 500, please have a discussion with your FRA.

And that, ladies and gentlemen, is the problem and the solution in a simplified example.

So, with regard to the equity portion of your investments, one crucial part of the FRA's job, once you are set on the path to your goals, is to make sure you do not get scared and sell out. Most people *do* get scared out (see Dalbar chart page 119). OH…. and you are retired…..see the Dalbar chart again. This is why I am so adamant about finding and hiring the FRA and not going it alone. MOST of us are going to need growth of our monies in retirement years; it is part of the overall plan of being a good steward of your money.

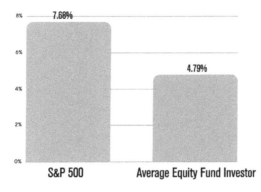

Source: "Quantitative Analysis of Investor Behavior, Key Findings from 2016" DALBAR, Inc. www.dalbar.com As of the time of this book, this is the latest QAIB study from DALBAR, Inc.

You need to fully understand that by holding a high-quality diversified stock portfolio throughout your 20 to 30 years of retirement, you should get a good return. But every five years or so (note, no one on this planet can time it consistently), on average, the market will crash. It is very volatile, but don't make the mistake of getting out. And you could swear up and down that you won't get out, but I have learned over the past 22 years in this business that you can't make the best decisions until you have a Functional Retirement Advisor to help you.

CHAPTER 14

FEES
WHAT ARE YOU PAYING
FOR, AND WHY?

No man is so wise that he can afford to wholly ignore the advice of others.

— James Lendall Basford (1845–1915),
Sparks from the Philosopher's Stone, 1882

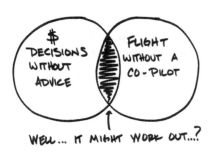

Now that you have the criteria for the FRA, let's talk about how the FRA makes their money.

Advisors charge in various ways. Many people prefer fee-based advisors to those who are commission based because those fees are somewhat linked to the client's account performance, meaning that when you do well, your advisor does well and everybody wins. Furthermore, the current conventional wisdom or "witch-hunt" out there is that commission-based advisors are often tempted to push certain investments over others because they come with higher commissions. But in reality, it almost doesn't matter what your advisor's compensation structure is as long as he's completely open and honest about it, both up front and along the way. If you're well aware of how much you're paying your advisor, it means you're dealing with someone who believes in transparency.[17]

What does a Functional Retirement Advisor provide for you? What do they do? What are you paying for? I have learned the three parts that a good Functional Retirement Advisor would be providing from another mentor I used in my career named Barry LaValley, the founder of The Retirement Lifestyle Center. The Retirement Lifestyle Center is a research and education company focusing on the key issues associated with retirement today. The company helps North Americans and their advisors and coaches redefine the traditional view of retirement and create a plan that is more in keeping with 21st century retirement.

I first met Barry at a 2009 broker-dealer conference where he was a featured speaker. He amazed me with how

---

17 www.fool.com/investing/general/2016/05/21/5-signs-you-can-trust-your-financial-advisor.aspx

he tied together lifestyle and money. I always recognized that you should get to know the person first before you talk about their finances, but Barry showed me how to get to the heart of that practice.

Barry was a consultant to me for many years and is one of my confidants to this day. Thanks to his influence, Falbo Wealth Management holds bi-monthly workshops for potential and current clients that feature a mix of financial and lifestyle professionals to talk on a variety of topics pertinent to retirees. Providing clients with access to this knowledge base has helped them—and me—with designing their retirement plan moving forward.

The biggest game-changer that Barry brought was helping me define three key words that I wanted my practice to live by, which is clarity, insight, and partnership.

Clarity Insight Partnership

CLARITY. "People don't know what they don't know." How much confusion is out there in the retirement planning world? We are bombarded by so many different products and strategies and gurus from everywhere. A Functional Retirement Advisor provides clarity to your situation.

They make it clear to you, based on your circumstances, what you should be doing and not doing. What should worry and stress you and what should not. For example, clients come to us thinking they need long-term-care insurance, and after going through their plan and understanding their financial and life position, it makes sense for them to self-insure for long-term-care insurance. Or the opposite happens—people come in thinking they don't need long-term-care insurance, and guess what? They do need it. People come in saying they don't want to take any risk, but meanwhile they have all their retirement savings in one stock, in one company—the company where they worked for 30 years. Some might argue that that could possibly be the riskiest retirement portfolio you can have. Then there are other people who come in thinking they need to take more risk yet they need to take *less* risk. Others coming in thinking they can't or shouldn't take any risk, but discover that to get to their goals, they have to step it up a little in risk, they need to be educated about risk and so on and so on. A good Functional Retirement Advisor provides CLARITY. Make sure the FRA has a clear and realistic view of your future, and *you* have a clear and realistic view of your future.

INSIGHT. The meaning to this is twofold. One is the Functional Retirement Advisor's experience; their insight into retirement and financial planning. I recommend no less than 15 to 20 years of helping individuals in financial planning, which should equate to their having helped many, many people in retirement and through retirement.

It also should mean they have gone through one or maybe two huge bear markets. You should benefit from their experience: It's not the first time they have helped someone in retirement, yet it will be your first and probably only time retiring. They have done training in their career, like, for example, the two years of CFP training along with the rigorous test and the 30 hours of continuing education every two years. The second part of INSIGHT is their insight into you as a person, understanding you as a person.

PARTNERSHIP. A Functional Retirement Advisor should be a good partner to you, which means they will be with you every step of the way. There should be some sort of ongoing reviews, but in my opinion, quarterly reviews are overkill. They wind up becoming counterproductive because the discussion becomes about performance, which is the wrong thing to focus on. There should be semiannual to annual reviews, depending. You must realize that you will go through all sorts of life transitions, and once again, that will be the first time you are going through this transition. Retirement, grandchildren, vacations, downsizing, relocating to a new state, launching a second career, going through a divorce, experiencing different stages of health, losing a spouse to illness and death, possibly getting remarried, coming to the rescue to help your children, grandchildren and even your parents out if they need it, and eventually your own death. This is all something the seasoned Functional Retirement Advisor has seen before through his clients and has helped his clients through over the years. That goes hand-in-hand with the economic financial cycles of bull markets straight to manic high markets right back to recessions and depressions and bear markets.

That is what you are paying a Functional Retirement Advisor for. According to Nick Murray, you are paying an advisor to accomplish three things:

1. Over time, you are looking to, hopefully, get at least (example 1% a year charge) 1% or more in return than you would over your lifetime by yourself. Now that doesn't mean that at any time it's about out-performing. An FRA would not talk about out-performance. It just means you will be acting and behaving the way you should over your investment lifetime to get at least 1% or better in return.

2. Ensure that you won't make the mistakes most people make over their investment lifetimes that can easily cost you in excess of 1% a year.

3. All the other stuff that goes with helping you: the reporting, the rebalancing, checking out the investments, the planning, regular service, with-drawals and any questions you have along the way. Basically, taking the stress out of it for you and making it a better investment experience.

How the Advisor Gets Paid for His Services

There is diversification in that your assets should be spread out among stocks, bonds and cash. Then there is tax diversi-fication by having your money invested in taxable accounts, tax-deferred accounts as well as tax-free accounts. And then there is diversification among fee-based business and com-mission. Yes, fee-based business is great, and yes, there are times when commission-based is a great strategy to use for the client. Your Functional Retirement Advisor, in my opinion, should be offering both. There are times when fee-based makes sense, there are times when commission-based makes sense and there are times when both make sense. I believe that the hybrid model of fees and commission is the best! If all the selection criteria fit, your FRA will do the right thing for you. Even on the commission side, he will explain what his model is and whether his is a "hybrid" model. Have a conversation about fee-based, commission-based, fee only and commission only, and you will be more educated and more confident.

As of the date of this book, the hybrid model is still allowed. The rules are still uncertain, though, and in the future regulators might allow only fee-based or commission-based business. They could even make it so regulated to do commission-based that no advisor will want to do it. There is even talk that commission-based products may become fee-based products. My belief is that if you have an FRA, it won't matter which strategy they use *once they have the plan done* and know you as a person first. Remember, the fee-only model is not a 100% lock that they have your best interest in mind before theirs. Make sure they meet the criteria in this book, and all else should fall in place.

A client might say, "But I don't want to pay when my account is down with the market." Then the FRA will explain, "Of course you don't want to pay, you are down in account value." And then he explains how it affects both parties. The reasoning is that the FRA is taking a pay cut, and during times of high market stress, they will be taking a hefty pay cut, working longer hours and having harder conversations. In essence, the advisor earns less as you pay less, since you are paying a percentage. As your account earns more, the advisor earns more and you pay more.

Compare it like this. If you buy commercial real estate, not looking at the account balance constantly helps you not to panic. Your rents are still coming in when the real estate market is down, but you will be paying insurance and maintenance on the properties. You will also be paying property tax, which happens whether the price of the property goes up or down. Yes, the property value can go down—it does happen, and most people don't realize that because they don't check their prices on real estate constantly. A 1% fee on assets being run by a Functional Retirement Advisor plus whatever extra fees for the funds and custodian—let's call it all in 1.6%—is worth every dime and multiples of what you will pay for good, competent, functional, congruent advice.

Like anything else, if you do not think all of this is worth what you are paying for and you honestly do not see the value in it, don't do it.

CHAPTER 15

THE BOTTOM LINE

"Yesterday I was clever. So I wanted to change the world. Today I am wise so I am changing myself"

— Rumi

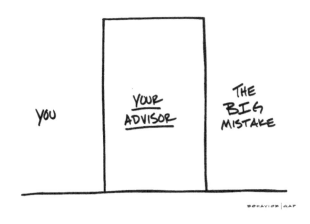

Finally, let's address the do-it-yourselfers and the new robo advisor companies. I do believe that the new systems for financial software and correlating technology is amazing. I also believe it will eventually put a dent in the workings of, let's say, a Chartered Financial Analyst (CFA) and change the landscape a bit. A computer will be able to do a stock analyst's job better than a human, so the actual planning software will get better and better. However, *I do not believe you* will ever get the best financial plan doing it yourself.

I don't watch television much these days, but when I do, I like to watch sports on TV. I notice during my New York Giants games that there are commercials picking on financial advisors. These, of course, come from the companies that say you can do it all yourself and don't need a financial advisor's help. They actually "warn" viewers to be careful when working with advisors.

First of all, a very small segment of the financial advisor population is this untrustworthy. Are there financial advisors like this? Of course; the few ruin it for the entire bunch. These unfair stereotypes portrayed in these paid advertisements are forcing people to think that all financial advisors are like used-car salesmen. Companies are taking advantage of viewers' naiveté saying, "Hey, you'd better do investment and planning yourself!" Unfortunately, retirement isn't that easy, as you saw in the 21st-century retirement landscape I summarize in Chapter 3. As a matter of fact, it is going to be very challenging, and it will continue to get more so without a competent Functional Retirement Advisor.

But, let me be clear on this. I believe there are too many moving parts and emotions to do it yourself. There are too many different choices and avenues the client can choose from (and most people, in my experience, cannot do all of them, for there is only a limited amount of capital). The Functional Retirement Advisor will help with deciding which roads to take and which choices you may have to leave behind. Then there's also the help you would get emotionally to stomach the swinging of the markets and economies, as well as everything that life will throw at you, which I call life transitions. The human being is an emotional creature, and left to his own desires with his own monies, he usually makes really bad decisions at really bad times.

Emotional Cycle of Investing

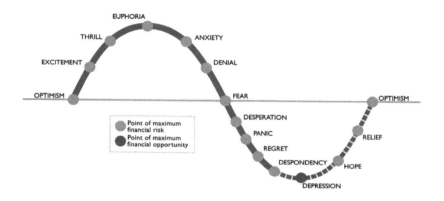

Source: TCI FOUNDATION www.tci-foundation.
org/the-herd/emotional-cycle-of-investing-2

The chart above represents the hypothetical tracking of investments
made. As the price goes up and down we see certain emotions that
are typical of an investor's emotions. These emotions in turn trigger
an almost irresistible impulse to buy and sell at exactly the wrong
moment. Just when we and everyone around us are tempted to give
up in disgust, that may be the point of maximum opportunity.
Likewise, when the market has gone up for several periods in a row
and we are all giddy, we may be at the point of maximum risk.[18]

While do-it-yourself active trading can be fun and give
you a sense of control, it may not translate into profits.
Fact: Individual investors tend to underperform the

18 https://www.forbes.com/sites/greatspeculations/2012/10/18/
understand-the-cycle-of-market-emotions-to-make-better-investing-
decisions/#1c891e337f48

market. Many studies have been done on this phenomenon, such as professors Brad Barber and Terrance Odean's published work. They have devoted well over a decade to studying how individuals invest. One of their most well-known studies, "Trading Is Hazardous to Your Wealth: The Common Stock Performance of Individual Investors," concluded that the average individual investor underperformed a market index by 1.5% a year. The same study also demonstrated that active traders underperformed by 6.5% annually.[19] Let's face it most new people who come into my office are just one big mistake from blowing up and screwing up their entire retirement. All it takes is one BIG mistake—mistakes people are making on their own all the time.

Mistakes like: selling at the bottom of the markets or going all in on the latest technology company ala 1999 at the top of the markets, or putting more money than they should on hot Florida real estate in 2006. In my view, it is too emotional and we need a third party that is not emotionally attached to the monies as much. It is the first time the person is retiring, the first time they are dealing with a real bad market in retirement, the first time they are dealing with the death of a spouse. For the Functional Retirement Advisor, it is not the first time they will be seeing these situations. They will have experience with the situation that goes along with having the credentials and training that most lay people just simply don't have. The Functional Retirement Advisor has helped hundreds of people with and through retirement. It comes down to the fact that I do find the tech and software amazing and I do think in the

19 https://www.forbes.com/sites/jamescahn/2014/03/05/why-and-how-to-choose-a-financial-advisor/#6ecca54bf06b

long run it will help the advisors do an even better job than possible with the QUANtitative data, however, it will always be a slight edge for the client to have a Functional Retirement Advisor utilizing their experience and the QUALitative data tied to the money.

Bottom line, this book will help you avoid the advisors portrayed in bad commercials and ads. It will also help you from working with a dysfunctional retirement advisor— someone who doesn't meet my criteria. They are not necessarily bad advisors or out to do harm, they are just not up to the optimal Functional Retirement Advisor standard I am talking about. You need—and deserve—the right partner for your retirement lifestyle goals. As Barry LaValley says, "Tying money to life."

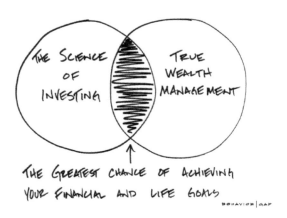

ACKNOWLEDGMENTS

I'd like to thank my clients for trusting me to help shape their retirement lives. These relationships are a huge reason why I continue to love what I do.

I want to thank those who have helped me grow and evolve in my career—Nick Murray, Barry LaValley, George Kinder and my financial advisor coach, Joe Lukacs.

Sydney LeBlanc, thank you for patience, guidance and wisdom in transforming my words into a legitimate guide for 21st century retirees. Joanne Camas and Mickey Andreko, I appreciate your mastery of proofreading. Damonza.com, thank you for creating an aesthetically pleasing product. Carl Richards of Behavior Gap—thank you for your sketches, which brought to life some of the main points I wanted to drive home.

Thank you to my loving fiancé, Lisa Marie Latino, for showing me that you can write a book by doing one herself. Your phenomenal talent was the driving force that brought this project to completion.

BIO

Joseph F. Falbo, Jr. is a Certified Financial Planner (CFP), an Accredited Investment Fiduciary (AIF), a Certified Retirement Counselor (CRC) and a Registered Life Planner (RLP).

Joseph has always been interested in people, money and how the two fit together. Upon graduating from St. John's University in 1995, he completed Merrill Lynch's Financial Advisor training program. Joseph has worked for a number of large brokerage firms and banks as a financial advisor, including Wachovia/Wells Fargo and Merrill Lynch.

In 2009, Joseph launched Falbo Wealth Management in New Providence, New Jersey. Falbo Wealth is an independent financial planning firm geared toward helping people *to* and *through* retirement, and where Joseph currently practices.

APPENDIX

Sample Nondisclosure Agreement

BASIC NONDISCLOSURE AGREEMENT

This Nondisclosure Agreement (the "Agreement") is entered into by and between _____ with its principal offices at _____, ("Disclosing Party") and

_____, located at _____ ("Receiving Party") for the purpose of preventing the unauthorized disclosure of Confidential Information as defined below. The parties agree to enter into a confidential relationship with respect to the disclosure of certain proprietary and confidential information ("Confidential Information").

1. Definition of Confidential Information. For purposes of this Agreement, "Confidential Information" shall include all information or material that has or could have commercial value or other utility in the business in which Disclosing Party is engaged. If Confidential Information is in written form, the Disclosing Party shall label or stamp the materials with the word "Confidential" or some similar warning. If Confidential Information is transmitted

orally, the Disclosing Party shall promptly provide a writing indicating that such oral communication constituted Confidential Information.

2. Exclusions from Confidential Information. Receiving Party's obligations under this Agreement do not extend to information that is: (a) publicly known at the time of disclosure or subsequently becomes publicly known through no fault of the Receiving Party; (b) discovered or created by the Receiving Party before disclosure by Disclosing Party; (c) learned by the Receiving Party through legitimate means other than from the Disclosing Party or Disclosing Party's representatives; or (d) is disclosed by Receiving Party with Disclosing Party's prior written approval.

3. Obligations of Receiving Party. Receiving Party shall hold and maintain the Confidential Information in strictest confidence for the sole and exclusive benefit of the Disclosing Party. Receiving Party shall carefully restrict access to Confidential Information to employees, contractors and third parties as is reasonably required and shall require those persons to sign nondisclosure restrictions at least as protective as those in this Agreement. Receiving Party shall not, without prior written approval of Disclosing Party, use for Receiving Party's own benefit, publish, copy, or otherwise disclose to others, or permit the use by others for their benefit or to the detriment of Disclosing Party, any Confidential Information. Receiving Party shall return to Disclosing Party any and all records, notes, and other written, printed,

or tangible materials in its possession pertaining to Confidential Information immediately if Disclosing Party requests it in writing.

4. Time Periods. The nondisclosure provisions of this Agreement shall survive the termination of this Agreement and Receiving Party's duty to hold Confidential Information in confidence shall remain in effect until the Confidential Information no longer qualifies as a trade secret or until Disclosing Party sends Receiving Party written notice releasing Receiving Party from this Agreement, whichever occurs first.

5. Relationships. Nothing contained in this Agreement shall be deemed to constitute either party a partner, joint venturer or employee of the other party for any purpose.

6. Severability. If a court finds any provision of this Agreement invalid or unenforceable, the remainder of this Agreement shall be interpreted so as best to effect the intent of the parties.

7. Integration. This Agreement expresses the complete understanding of the parties with respect to the subject matter and supersedes all prior proposals, agreements, representations and understandings. This Agreement may not be amended except in a writing signed by both parties.

8. Waiver. The failure to exercise any right provided in this Agreement shall not be a waiver of prior or subsequent rights.

9. Notice of Immunity [OPTIONAL]

Employee is provided notice that an individual shall not be held criminally or civilly liable under any federal or state trade secret law for the disclosure of a trade secret that is made (i) in confidence to a federal, state, or local government official, either directly or indirectly, or to an attorney; and (ii) solely for the purpose of reporting or investigating a suspected violation of law; or is made in a complaint or other document filed in a lawsuit or other proceeding, if such filing is made under seal. An individual who files a lawsuit for retaliation by an employer for reporting a suspected violation of law may disclose the trade secret to the attorney of the individual and use the trade secret information in the court proceeding, if the individual (i) files any document containing the trade secret under seal; and (ii) does not disclose the trade secret, except pursuant to court order.

This Agreement and each party's obligations shall be binding on the representatives, assigns and successors of such party. Each party has signed this Agreement through its authorized representative.

_____ (Signature)

_____ (Typed or Printed Name)

Date: _____

_____ (Signature)

_____ (Typed or Printed Name)

Date: _____

DISCLOSURE

Securities and Advisory services offered through LPL Financial, a Registered Investment Advisor, Member FINRA/SIPC.

The opinions voiced in this material are for general information only and are not intended to provide specific advice or recommendations for any individual. All performance referenced is historical and is no guarantee of future results. All indices are unmanaged and may not be invested into directly

The Standard & Poor's 500 Index is a capitalization weighted index of 500 stocks designed to measure performance of the broad domestic economy through changes in the aggregate market value of 500 stocks representing all major industries.

All investing involves risk including loss of principal. No strategy assures success or protects against loss. There is no guarantee that a diversified portfolio will enhance overall returns or outperform a non-diversified portfolio. Diversification does not protect against market risk.

Fixed and Variable annuities are suitable for long-term investing, such as retirement investing. Gains from tax-deferred investments are taxable as ordinary income upon withdrawal. Guarantees are based on the claims paying ability of the issuing company. Withdrawals made prior to age 59 ½ are subject to a 10% IRS penalty tax and surrender charges may apply. Variable annuities are subject to market risk and may lose